MW00911821

Illustration /// Annemarie Buchner /// anibuchner@gmail.com
Graphic Design /// Kevin Pedersen /// Kevinprintsareus@gmail.com
Graphic Design /// Doug Pedersen /// contactdapperpress@gmail.com
Executive Director /// Melina Pedersen
Publisher – Book Baby
ISBN: 978-1-54390-498-7

TEARS OF GLORY

A story inspired by visions

DEDICATION

Lovingly dedicated to my wife Melina

and sons Douglas and Kevin

Jon a Judi,

Invite Christ into your
life and experience the
love in your heart,

Love,

Denny

TEARS OF GLORY

CHAPTER 1

It is a beautiful autumn day in Portland. The sky is blue, the air is cool, the wind swirls the beautiful colored leaves that have fallen from the trees, and all is good with the Adams' family. At dinner that evening, Joseph and Sarah are having their own private celebration, as they have just received the good news about their first pregnancy. Sarah is now about six weeks along and knows she has much planning and preparation to do before the big day. Joseph also knows he is going to be busy with the "Honey Do List" that Sarah will have for him, and he looks forward to being a father for the first time.

Joseph and Sarah are very happy, and the next seven months seem to just fly by. Finally, "D" (delivery) day arrives, and Joseph is in the delivery room with Sarah, holding her hand and giving her the limited instructions that he learned at the Lamaze classes they previously attended.

The Lamaze classes' goal is to increase the women's confidence in her ability to give birth. Sarah had chosen the Bradley Method, which embraces the idea that childbirth is a natural process and which, with the right preparation, could help the mother avoid pain medication and routine interventions during labor.

With all of Sarah's self-determination and Lamaze class teachings, the birthing process goes as well as can be expected. Sarah comes through delivery with no problems; it is Joseph who has to sit on the floor next to the delivery bed with his head between his legs, taking deep breaths so as not to pass out. The gynecologist, Dr. Lothridge, and attending nurses chuckle privately between themselves as they glance down at Joseph.

Soon after, Sarah is back in her room, smiling and sitting up in bed, and Joseph sits in a chair next to the window, still looking a little under the weather. Within about thirty minutes, their new family member is brought to Sarah, who has a beautiful glow about her that seems to brighten the room.

With weak and shaky legs, Joseph stands up and walks over to the bed to have his first look at their new son. He is a beautiful child and weighs seven pounds and eight ounces. He has little hair on his head, and his skin is as pink as can be.

Joseph takes Sarah's hand in his, kisses her on the cheek, and then kisses his new son on the forehead. Joseph and Sarah look at each other and, with their new son in Sarah's arms, begin to cry, as this is what life, love, and marriage is all about.

Joseph then says to Sarah, "We must now name our newborn son, a name that he will be proud of." They ponder a few names before agreeing on Gabriel. Gabriel is one of only two angels named in the Bible the other being Michael and his name means "strong man of God" or "God is my strength."

Still holding Sarah's hand, Joseph takes one of Gabriel's tiny hands in his and has Sarah take Gabriel's other hand, creating a circle of energy. Joseph then bows his head with Sarah and says a prayer in thanks to God, "Loving God, thank You for the gift of life and for bringing Gabriel safely into this world. May You bless him and keep him, helping him to grow loving, strong, and healthy in Your love, now and always. Amen."

Joseph and Sarah kiss their new son at the same time as tears flow from both of their eyes gently onto Gabriel's head. This time in their lives is certainly the happiest that life could ever offer.

CHAPTER 2

It is four weeks after Gabriel's birth, and today is another important time in their lives as Gabriel is to be baptized. At a private gathering at their church, all of their immediate family members and close friends are in attendance to witness this blessed event.

Holy baptism is the basis of the whole Christian life, the gateway to life in the Spirit. Through baptism, we are freed from sin and reborn as children of God. To baptize means to plunge or immerse into water and symbolizes dying and being buried with Christ. The action of coming out of the water indicates Christ's resurrection.

As all are seated in the church pews with Joseph, Sarah, Gabriel, and the chosen godparents, Pastor Maragelis enters the elevated altar, smiles, and looks down over the congregation, with around fifty in attendance. As he begins the ceremony, he welcomes and thanks everyone for attending this very important day in Gabriel's life. He goes on to tell why, at this time; Gabriel is to bond with Christ. Infants are born with a fallen human nature and are tainted with original sin; children also have need of the new birth in Baptism to be freed from the power of darkness and brought into the realm of freedom of the children of God.

After a few more words, he asks Joseph and Sarah to bring Gabriel to the baptismal and to be accompanied by the godparents as witnesses. As they are standing next to the baptismal, Sarah has Gabriel wrapped in her arms and dressed in fine linens. Pastor Maragelis then removes a portion of the linen cloth, exposing Gabriel's head and face. As he begins the baptismal prayer, he dips a gold leaf in the baptismal water and continues on with the prayer. He then slowly releases the water, which flows over the top of Gabriel's head.

At that exact moment, for some unknown reason, the pastor stops speaking in the middle of the prayer and stares down at Gabriel. As he makes eye contact with Gabriel, it is almost like he goes into a trance and cannot speak or take his eyes off him. While staring into Gabriel's eyes, he begins to have heavenly visions at lightning speed, and then it is as if his whole life flashes before him.

The next thing he recalls is lying on the floor, with Joseph and a couple of other people holding the back of his head and helping him to his feet. Joseph asks the pastor if he is okay, and he states that he doesn't recall having blacked out and that this has never happened to him before. Now totally embarrassed, Pastor Maragelis thanks Joseph and his friends for their assistance and says, "Let us please proceed with the baptism."

He again dips the gold leaf in the baptismal, slowly releases the water over Gabriel's head, and continues the prayer. This time, as the water touches the top of Gabriel's head, the pastor makes a concentrated effort not to look into Gabriel's eyes.

As he finishes the baptismal prayer, he glances down at Gabriel, and there before him, and also seen by Joseph, Sarah, and the godparents, is the sign of a Red Cross on his forehead. As they all stare at the cross, Sarah asks Pastor Maragelis, "What does this mean?"

The only explanation that immediately comes to his mind is that it must be just a birthmark. Joseph then states that this was not there before and it only appeared when the holy baptismal water had touched Gabriel's head. The pastor then states that in all honesty, he has no explanation except that it is truly incredible that this has just occurred.

A moment later, Pastor Maragelis says, "It must be a sign from God, but for what reason, I do not know." Shortly thereafter, the sign of the Red Cross vanishes from Gabriel's forehead.

CHAPTER 3

For the next five years, Gabriel develops normally, and Joseph and Sarah are very happy with their life. All seems to go as planned, with Sarah able to stay at home with Gabriel even though finances are limited with the family having only one income.

Gabriel is now old enough to attend kindergarten at a private Christian school, and Sarah is having a difficult time dealing with the thought of letting him go for the first time. Since Gabriel will soon be in school, Sarah starts a part-time job as a bookkeeper to help pay for the new expense.

Finally, the first day of school arrives, and both Joseph and Sarah accompany Gabriel to Kennedy School to meet his new teacher for the first time. Her name is Mrs. Jordan, and she has been a kindergarten teacher at the school now for around ten years. She is highly regarded at the school, and many parents have requested her to be their child's teacher. However, only twenty kids to a classroom are allowed.

As they walk into the classroom, Mrs. Jordan approaches them with a kindly smile and open hand to welcome them. She then gets down on one knee so as to be at eye level with Gabriel, gently grabs his hand, and says, "Hi, my name is Mrs. Jordan. What is your name?"

With his big brown eyes, Gabriel looks directly at Mrs. Jordan, smiles, and says, "My name is Gabriel."

Shortly thereafter, school is to begin, so Mrs. Jordan shows Gabriel where he is to sit. With an empty feeling in their stomachs, Joseph and teary-eyed Sarah say good-bye to Gabriel and leave the classroom.

Almost immediately after leaving, Sarah returns to the classroom, runs back to Gabriel, and says, "I love you, and I will be here to pick you up at the end of the day."

Gabriel smiles and says, "I love you too, Mommy," and gives her a big hug.

Gabriel is very excited about being in kindergarten and is not at all nervous. Seated next to Gabriel is Mary, a sweet, soft-spoken five-year-old with braided, blond hair and blue eyes. Her mother has dressed her in a pretty white chiffon dress and black patent shoes.

For the first hour, Gabriel and Mary do not speak much, as both are unfamiliar with someone their own age of the opposite sex. However, as the morning continues, at around 10:00 a.m., they are now becoming more comfortable with one another and share apple juice and granola bars at their recess.

As the day proceeds at recess, around 2:00 p.m., Gabriel and Mary are together on the playground, sharing an apple and playing as kids do. At that moment, a big kid from the third grade, along with all of his friends, walks over to them and becomes verbally aggressive. He is the school bully and has no regard for anyone except for himself.

He looks at Gabriel and Mary and says, "Give me your apple." Gabriel and Mary, not being accustomed to this type of aggressive behavior, stand there, not knowing what to do or say. Just then, the bully grabs the apple out of Mary's hand and starts to eat it. Mary says, "Give me back my apple! It is not yours."

The bully looks at his friends, and they all begin to smile, knowing quite well what is going to happen. The bully shoves Mary's shoulder, and she falls down on the ground, getting her dress dirty. The bully looks down at her and says, "Looks like it is my apple now."

Gabriel helps Mary to her feet, and she begins to cry from embarrassment and fear. Gabriel walks over to the bully without a word. He looks up at the bully and stares intensely into his eyes.

As the bully stares into Gabriel's eyes, he

seems to go into a trance, with a blank look on his face. Gabriel reaches up and puts his hand on the bully's right shoulder. With a tearful look, the bully slowly hands Gabriel the apple and walks off with his friends. Gabriel hands Mary the apple, asks her if she is okay, and they both walk back to their classroom. This particular act of Gabriel's would remain in Mary's memory forever.

CHAPTER 4

Through the next eight years, Gabriel and Mary remain good friends, and so do Gabriel's and Mary's parents, Tom and Pamela Hart. Often, the two families get together to play cards, share dinner at each other's house, and occasionally go to the beach or to the mountains for the weekend.

It is now towards the end of summer, and Grant High School, for both Gabriel and Mary, is to start soon. They are both excited, and Mary is somewhat nervous, which is a normal reaction. Gabriel, on the other hand, is curious about what challenges high school will bring; however, he is very calm, as this is his personality and nature. He typically is always in control of his actions and thinks out most situations before he reacts, which is uncommon for a teenager who is fourteen years of age.

Finally, the first day of high school arrives, and Gabriel and Mary walk to school together, as they live only one block apart and school is only five blocks from Mary's house. As the kids are all standing outside the school and socializing with their friends, Gabriel happens to notice an older student who is wearing his letterman's jacket walking by. The boy makes eye contact with Mary, and they both smile and acknowledge each other. Just then, the school bell rings, and all of the kids scramble to their assigned classes.

The first day of school goes quite well, and the last class of the day is history, which Gabriel and Mary have together. When the final school bell rings, Gabriel and Mary walk out of the classroom, into the hallway, and down toward their lockers, which are just ten feet apart. While they gather their books, the boy with the letterman's jacket stops at Mary's locker and introduces himself as Chad. Mary smiles at Chad and says, "Hi, my name is Mary."

At the sound of Mary's voice, Gabriel turns and notices that she is speaking to the same person that he saw earlier that day. Gabriel walks over to Mary's locker to see what is happening. Mary introduces him to Chad, and each acknowledges the other.

As the three walk down the hallway, they hear a commotion from the principal's office. Just then, they hear sirens outside the school and see firemen and paramedics rushing through the front doors. They enter the principal's office and see, there on the floor, lying on his back, Mr. Kleiner, the school principal. The paramedics begin to perform CPR, and then a defibrillator is used to try and restart his heart.

The paramedics work on Mr. Kleiner for several minutes but with no response. Finally, one of the paramedics states that the principal cannot be revived and it appears that he must have had a massive heart attack.

Gabriel, Mary, and Chad stand in the hallway, just outside the principal's office, observing everything. After a moment, Gabriel walks into the office, where everyone is very quiet and in shock. He walks up to the lifeless body, gets down on one knee, and grabs Mr. Kleiner's hand. Everyone in the room looks at Gabriel with puzzled expressions on their faces, not sure who he is or what he is doing. Gabriel bows his head, puts his right hand over Mr. Kleiner's heart, and begins to pray.

As he continues to pray, a fireman grabs Gabriel's arm and says, "Son, he is dead, and there is nothing anyone can do."

Gabriel does not react to the fireman but continues to kneel in deep concentration, with his head bowed, until, unnoticed by everyone, a Red Cross appears on his forehead and red tears of blood drop gently on the principal's face. Within seconds, Mr. Kleiner makes a groaning sound and moves his head. Gabriel sees his red tears on Mr. Kleiner's forehead and quickly wipes them away.

The paramedics quickly jump in and continue to perform CPR on Mr. Kleiner until he is breathing on his own. They then lift him on a gurney and secure him with safety straps.

As they head for the doorway, the fireman walks up to Gabriel, puts his hand on his shoulder, and gives him a big smile. They then wheel Mr. Kleiner out of the office, place him into the ambulance, turn on the siren, and depart for the hospital.

Gabriel walks into the hallway and says to Mary, "Let's go home."

Mary turns to Gabriel and says, "How did you do that?"

Gabriel looks at her with little expression and says nothing.

That evening, as Gabriel and his parents eat dinner, the telephone rings. Gabriel answers it and tells his mother that the call is for her. Sarah speaks to the caller, who is Mary's mother, Pamela, and who informs her about what happened at school that day.

Sarah walks back into the dining room, where Joseph and Gabriel are still eating, and asks Gabriel what happened at the principal's office. Gabriel is quiet and just looks at Sarah. Then he shrugs his shoulders and says, "The principal had a heart attack, and I felt that I must help him." Sarah continues to quiz Gabriel on what he did to assist the paramedics. Gabriel states that all he did was to pray that Mr. Kleiner might be saved.

Joseph and Sarah sit at the dinner table and stare at each other, wondering what really did happen and how Gabriel could have possibly assisted the paramedics, as he has never had any medical training.

CHAPTER 5

It is the next day at school, and Gabriel is at his first class. Two district school administrators walk into the classroom and ask his teacher to identify Gabriel, as they want to speak with him. As the two men approach Gabriel, they ask him to please step into the hallway. They lead him into an empty classroom and say they would like to ask him a few questions.

The men identify themselves as investigators with the school district and ask him for a statement regarding the incident that happened the previous day with the school principal. Gabriel tells the men what he had observed but leaves out the part about how he personally revived the principal.

One of the men then says, "We were told that you had performed some kind of medical procedure on Mr. Kleiner that revived him. Is that true?" Without answering the question, Gabriel asks if he is going to be okay.

The investigator replies, "He went through open-heart surgery, is in intensive care, and is expected to make a full recovery. My question again to you is how did you revive Mr. Kleiner? Both the paramedics and firemen indicated his heart had stopped and they could not resuscitate him. Actually, he was dead."

Gabriel says, "There was no medical procedure, as I know nothing about medicine. All I did was pray for him, and he must not have been dead as the paramedics thought."

The two men look at each other and appear to still be puzzled as to how Gabriel saved Mr. Kleiner's life. "Well, son, whatever happened yesterday, you have saved his life. We are still unsure of what happened; however, we only know that Mr. Kleiner is a very lucky man and extremely fortunate that you were there. On behalf of Mr. Kleiner and his family, I personally want to thank you for your participation."

Gabriel gives the man a smile and then says, "You know it was not I that saved Mr. Kleiner. It was just not his time yet. He is a good man and believes in Jesus as his Savior. He obviously has more work to do on this earth before he meets his maker."

The investigator then says, "How do you know he is a religious man?"

Gabriel replies, "He and his family belong to the same church that my family attends, and my parents are friends with them."

The men now stand, smile, and shake Gabriel's hand and thank him for his time. Gabriel returns to his class and finishes the school day. As Gabriel and

Mary are walking out of the school, a group of newscasters with their microphones and cameras approach them.

The newscasters start asking Gabriel numerous questions about yesterday. Gabriel states, "I had little to do with what happened, and you should be talking with the paramedics and firemen, as they are the true heroes." After a couple more questions, Gabriel excuses himself and continues to walk home with Mary.

At dinner that evening, Joseph, Sarah, and Gabriel are watching the local nightly news, and there on the screen is Gabriel being interviewed. Sarah says, "Look, Gabe, it appears that you are becoming a celebrity."

As they all watch the short interview, Gabriel doesn't say a word and is slightly embarrassed watching himself and observing his own appearance and listening to his own voice.

Joseph then asks Gabriel, "Just what really did happen?"

Gabriel then explains, "It was as if a voice was telling me to go to Mr. Kleiner and say a prayer for him. As I was praying for him, my body was tingling, and it was as if everything was happening in slow motion. I know that as I was praying, I had a heavenly vision, and it was if I could see Jesus' face in my mind.

Then, in an instant, it was all over."

Joseph and Sarah now make eye contact and say nothing, as they know that Gabriel is a special person and knew that from the day of his baptism and the appearance of a cross on his forehead. Actually, they have been waiting all these years to see if there was any significance to the holy sign, and now it is becoming apparent that Gabriel has a gift and this now just might be the beginning of things to come.

CHAPTER 6

The next nine months of school just seem to fly by for Gabriel and Mary. They both excel with good grades, and Gabriel is a straight-A student. They also make a lot of new friends.

Mary and Chad have dated a few times and are more like good friends rather than a couple, even though Chad would prefer that the relationship become more intimate. Often, the three go out and hang around together, as Gabriel and Chad has also become friends, even though Chad is a senior hanging around with a freshman. Gabriel, however, does not act like a freshman but is reserved and precocious and seems to have a direction for his life in mind. Mary, on the other hand, is popular at school, carefree, has a bubbly personality, and always seems to have a smile on her face.

It is now the end of May, Chad's senior prom is quickly approaching, and he asks Mary to be his date for the evening, which is a big deal for Mary considering she is only a freshman. Her parents agree that she can attend the dance, as they have come to know Chad as a nice and respectful young man and feel confident that he can be trusted with Mary.

It is now the evening of the prom and Gabriel

comes over to Mary's house to wish her a good time. As Gabriel runs up the stairway to Mary's room, he opens her door, and there stands Mary as pretty as can be and looking all grown up with her new dress and high heels, her hair styled, and her make-up on. Gabriel just stands there, staring at her, not saying a word, as he cannot believe his eyes. Mary is absolutely breathtaking, and for the first time, he sees her really as a woman rather than just a good friend that he has known all these years.

Mary looks at Gabriel, smiles, and says, "What do you think?"

As Gabriel looks at Mary, he doesn't know what to say and is actually mesmerized by her beauty. It is at that exact moment that Gabriel, for the first time in his life, actually feels a real sexual emotion for someone. Not wanting to appear to be silly or stupid, he mumbles, "You look fab." However, now that he is uptight with Mary's new appearance, he has trouble making his lips move, as each lip feels like it weighs five pounds, and it sounds like he says, "You look fat."

Mary looks at Gabriel and says in a loud voice, "Did you say I LOOK FAT?"

Gabriel, now red-faced, stutters his words: "No, Mary, I said you look fab, as in fabulous. Honest, you look great." Mary just stares at Gabriel. Then she smiles and says, "I was hoping that is what you said." After a couple of minutes, Gabriel says that he has to leave, and he wishes Mary the best time at the prom.

As he is leaving, a white limousine drives up in front of the house, and Chad gets out of the car, looking very dapper in his black tuxedo. Gabriel walks up to him and tells him how great he looks and says, "Wait till you see Mary. She is absolutely gorgeous."

As Chad walks up to the house with a corsage in hand, Gabriel then ducks behind some bushes and watches from a short distance. As Chad and Mary get into the limousine, he can see there are two other couples already inside and they are all happy and laughing. As the limousine drives off, the driver and Gabriel make eye contact, and Gabriel has this funny feeling. However, he dismisses it. Also, Gabriel gets a real empty feeling in his stomach, and a slight tear enters his eyes. He now knows for the first time in his life that he actually loves Mary and at this time can do nothing about it.

Gabriel then walks home, has dinner with his folks, and then decides to go up to his room and watch the new Harry Potter movie that has just arrived. He watches the movie, goes downstairs to gets some snacks, and then goes back up to his room, and after a couple of minutes, he decides to retire early.

At around midnight, Gabriel is sound asleep, and then all of a sudden, he sits straight up in bed and has this awful feeling that something has happened to Mary. He puts his clothes on and heads over to Mary's house to see if everything is all right.

As he approaches the house, all of the lights are on, and for some unknown reason, he senses that something is wrong and runs up to the house. As he looks in the window, he can see Tom and Pamela Hart frantically running around, and then the automatic garage door opens. Gabriel runs over to the garage and sees Mr. Hart get into the car and begin to pull the car out of the garage. Gabriel then looks in the car window, sees the stressed look on Mr. Hart's face, and knocks on the car window. Mr. Hart puts the window down and just looks at Gabriel.

Gabriel says, "Is everything okay, Mr. Hart? You look as if something is wrong."

Tom states, "Mary and all the kids in the limousine have been in a bad accident, and I must get over there right now."

Just then, Pamela Hart comes running out of the house, attempting to put on her coat. Gabriel says that he must go with them and jumps into the back seat. Within a couple of minutes, which seem much longer to Gabriel, they arrive at the scene of the accident and see many police cars, three ambulances, and two fire trucks, with all their emergency lights flashing.

A few yards behind the vehicles, and partially blocked from view, is the white limousine. It looks like a bulldozer has hit it. As Gabriel and Mary's parents get out of the car and walk closer to the limousine, they can see paramedics with stretchers and firemen trying to get into the limousine. Two people are still pinned in the vehicle, and they can't get them out due to the crushed and mangled steel and metal that entraps them.

Gabriel now has this sick feeling in his stomach and knows that Mary is one of the people that is trapped in the vehicle. Unseen, he quickly ducks under the yellow warning tape and walks right past a policeman and looks in the limousine window. It is difficult seeing anything due to the disfigured interior of the vehicle and also because it is dark. As he puts his face closer to the side window of the limousine, he squints, and his eyes are drawn to a certain area on the floor. He then makes eye contact with Mary as she is looking directly at him. The rest of her body cannot be seen from this viewpoint. However, Gabriel knows that it is Mary. Then, right after that, Mary's eyes shut, and she cannot again be seen.

Gabriel calls over to one of the firemen and tells him what he has seen and where she is located. A couple of policemen then walk over to Gabriel and escort him back behind the yellow warning tape as they bring in the hydraulic-powered cutting and spreading tools (jaws of life) that can cut through steel and metal. This process takes some time, as they must be very careful as not to accidentally harm the two people that are still imprisoned in the vehicle.

As they are cutting through the steel and metal, they finally find the first person that is lying face down on the back seat. As they get to this person, the body is unrecognizable due to the severe damage. However, he is still breathing. They then get the body out of the limousine, put him on a stretcher, and wheel him towards the ambulance. There is still one more person in the vehicle, and it is Mary.

As the firemen continue to work and slowly remove portions of the vehicle, they finally see her feet and a portion of her legs up to the knees. They continue to make slow progress, and finally, they can see Mary's entire body. Her body appears to be crushed, and she is lifeless.

As they carefully remove her body from the vehicle, she is put on a stretcher and placed in an ambulance, which rapidly departs with sirens blaring. Gabriel then runs over to Mr. and Mrs. Hart. They get into their car and head off to the hospital. Gabriel tries to console the Harts, telling them that he made eye contact with Mary and that he thinks that she may still be alive. From that moment on, not another word is spoken by anyone until they enter the emergency room waiting area.

As they go to the front counter, they identify who they are to the nurse, who asks them to take a seat and tells them they will be contacted as soon as they know anything. As they are sitting in the emergency room lobby, Pamela Hart begins to cry uncontrollably, and Tom Hart is concerned for her. He talks to the attending nurse, who then takes Pamela inside the emergency room, has her lay down on one of the beds, and administers a sedative.

After about two hours, one of the emergency room surgical doctors walks up to Tom Hart and Gabriel and says, "I am sincerely sorry. We did all we could. However, every bone in Mary's body was broken, she had internal bleeding, and she could not be saved."

A look of extreme shock, sorrow and disbelief appears on Tom's face, and it is as if he has become numb. He then asks to be taken to Pamela's bedside, and as he explains the outcome to her, a scream of intense sorrow can be heard throughout the entire emergency room area.

Gabriel, still sitting in his seat in the emergency room waiting area, is also in shock, and his mind is racing with intense depression. Approximately thirty minutes later, Tom and Pamela Hart leave the hospital and return home. Gabriel does not join them and stays at the hospital, trying to figure out what happened. Information from the nurse indicates that it was Chad that they also had to cut out of the limousine, and that the other five occupants in the car were badly injured but should survive the accident. It seems that the limousine driver had been drinking and was at fault, as he was trying to beat a train at the crossing at sixty miles per hour. However, he lost the race.

CHAPTER 7

Gabriel remains at the hospital for about an hour longer and then decides to go down to the morgue. As he enters the morgue area, the overhead lights are dimmed, but he can still see the examination stainless steel tables all set up in a row. It is after hours, and the medical examiner does not come on duty until around 8:00 a.m. Gabriel is not sure why he is down in the morgue, only that he heard a voice in his head that led him here.

He looks around the room and then walks up to the stainless steel wall where the bodies are refrigerated and entombed and awaiting their turn for autopsy. He walks back and forth in front of the wall, finally stopping in front of one particular unit at waist height. As he stands there, he reaches out for the handle before pulling his hand back, thinking, what am I doing here? This is insane. But he doesn't move. It is like he is frozen where he stands, staring at this particular unit.

He again reaches out, grabs the handle, turns it downward, and then hears the click as the locking mechanism releases. Gabriel opens the unit door, and, automatically, the stainless steel table slowly moves out of the unit right in front of him and then stops.

Gabriel looks down on the corpse. It is covered with a white sheet, and he cannot see the hidden body. With shaky hands, Gabriel removes the sheet, exposing the face and neck area. There, he sees Mary's face, which is white and lifeless, but also peaceful. It is remarkable, considering how violently her body was thrown around in the car, that Mary's face was untouched.

Gabriel just stands there and looks down on Mary, not knowing what to think or how to react. After a short time, Gabriel's eyes begin to fill with tears, which slowly trickle down both cheeks. As he looks down at Mary, his eyes are so filled with tears that he cannot now even see her face. He begins to cry out loud and cannot control his sorrow, as he has never had such emptiness in his stomach and such a feeling of loss and depression. He wipes his eyes, allowing him to better view Mary, puts his right hand on Mary's cold forehead, and, with his left hand, grabs Mary's hand that is under the sheet. Gabriel begins to pray, but it is difficult for him to think, as his mind is filled with great sorrow and loss.

As he finally contains himself, he again begins to pray and says, "Lord our God, You are always faithful and quick to show mercy. Mary was suddenly taken from us. Please, come swiftly to her aid and grant me the power to bring Mary back into this earth so she may become one of Your chosen children to aid in supporting Your word and to be my mortal and earthly partner to give me strength so that I may be able to also teach the non-believers and strengthen the believers that You are the only way to true salvation and everlasting life. Christ, I ask in your name. Amen."

With bowed head, tear-filled eyes, and in deep concentration, Gabriel stands looking down on Mary's face. Within a split second, the sign of the Red Cross now appears on Gabriel's forehead, and his red tears of blood gently fall onto Mary's face.

As he is holding Mary's hand, he feels a slight twitch and believes it is his hand that made the sudden involuntary movement. Then, again, there is another twitch. However, it is a slightly stronger sensation this time. Gabriel, even though he is somewhat startled at what he thinks might now be happening, squeezes her hand, and immediately a strong response from Mary's hand is felt.

Gabriel's mind is now racing and thinking that he must be losing it, as how could her cold, lifeless body react to a simple squeezing of her hand? Gabriel now places his right hand over Mary's heart and puts his left hand on her forehead.

As this is happening, he again bows his head and asks God for the power to return Mary back to life. As Gabriel is standing over Mary's body, it is like he is having an out-of-body experience (in a trance like state, if you will) and is actually looking down upon himself and Mary, and he sees a glowing light hovering over Mary's body. As Gabriel is still standing over Mary, her face now turns to a normal pinkish color, there is a warmth to her forehead, and a movement received in her chest, and then a gasping, breathing sound is heard.

As Gabriel is looking down on Mary, he sees her beautiful blue eyes slowly open, and they make immediate eye contact. However, her eyes are still out of focus. As Mary is looking up, within a short period of time, she realizes it is Gabriel that is standing over her, and a slight, gentle smile appears on her face.

Gabriel, with tears in his eyes, smiles back at Mary and says, "Welcome home."

Mary, still lying down, turns her head in both directions, trying to figure out where she is. She then says to Gabriel, "Where am I?" As she begins to sit up to get a better perspective on where she is, Gabriel supports her back with his hand, as she is weak and still lightheaded. As Mary is now sitting up on the stainless steel table, she looks around the room and now realizes where she is.

She begins to cry out and says, "What am I

doing down in the morgue?"

Gabriel takes her hand and says, "Mary, you were in a terrible car accident, and you were pronounced dead. Do you not remember anything of the incident?"

Mary answers, "The last thing I remember is that we had left the prom, had dinner at Tiffany's restaurant, and were headed home. Other than that, I can't remember anything." She then asks about Chad and the other kids in the car, and Gabriel indicates that they are upstairs in serious condition but are all expected to live.

Mary now scoots herself off the table and stands. However, she is still a little weak, and Gabriel grabs her so she does not fall. Mary now says that she wants to get out of the morgue, to put on her own clothes and go home. Gabriel helps her walk to the elevator and pushes the up button. As they arrive at the main floor to the emergency room lobby, Gabriel walks Mary over to the seating area and has her sit down. As he does, the other people in the waiting area are all observing and wondering, "Why is this girl just wearing a white sheet and in her bare feet?" Gabriel tells Mary to stay put and he will be right back. He walks back into the emergency room and looks for her prom dress and shoes.

As he is looking around for her clothes, he sees

a bag with Mary's name on it, looks in the bag, and recognizes her dress. Gabriel now walks over to the door and signals Mary to come to him. Mary goes into a vacant room and puts her dress and shoes on. As she observes her dress in the mirror, she sees that it has been torn, and she also sees bloodstains on the front and sides.

As Mary exits the room, she walks into the hallway, where Gabriel is waiting. Just then, an emergency room doctor walks by, the same doctor that told Mr. Hart that Mary had died. He just stands there, looking at Mary in disbelief, and he has a look on his face as if he has just seen a ghost.

"What in the...?"

He then walks right up to Mary, grabs her hand, says, "Come with me," and calls out for one of the attending nurses to assist him. As they walk into one of the vacant exam rooms, he has Mary sit on the table so he can examine her, and then he asks Gabriel to remain in the hallway or waiting room area. Just before the exam room door is closed, one additional doctor and nurse hurriedly enter the room and then shut the door. Periodically, for the next hour, different doctors and nurses come in and out of the room, and Gabriel is getting a little restless just standing in the hallway. However, he is not going to leave Mary.

Finally, the door opens, and he hears laughter from the attending doctors and also hears Mary's own cute little chuckle that he knows so well. The attending doctor then walks out of the room, walks up to Gabriel, and looks him straight in the eye and says, "Young man, I don't know how this happened, but this is truly a miracle. I have heard and read of miracles occasionally occurring in the world, though none as miraculous as this one. When Mary was initially brought into the emergency room, she was actually dead. However, her brain was still slightly functioning, and we could not pronounce her dead until her brain ceased to function. In addition, all of the bones in her body were broken. Finally, she was pronounced dead." He then asks Gabriel if he has any information on how this could have happened.

Gabriel just stands there, staring at the doctor, and says nothing. The doctor then states, "This one is surely going to be in all of the medical and religious journals, and Mary is going to become very popular, as the newspapers and television stations are going to really publicize this story. I don't pretend to understand it, but supreme intervention has surely occurred, and the good Lord was not ready to receive her." The doctor then walks down the hallway, smiling and shaking his head, still in disbelief.

The hospital has now just released Mary and nurses ask her if they should call her parents. Mary says, "No thank you." However, she asks if she and Gabriel could be given a ride home.

As they arrive at Mary's house, Gabriel helps her out of the courtesy car and walks her up to the front door. Mary then gets a key from a hidden spot located under the front porch planter and opens the door. She then asks Gabriel to accompany her when she awakens her parents. As they enter the house, it is dark and quiet and has a feeling of emptiness and sorrow that only Gabriel can sense.

As they walk up to the second level, where her parents are, the stairs make a squeaking sound, and it is impossible to be absolutely quiet. They walk to her parent's bedroom and open the door. There, in the dark, with the full moon shining through the windows, they can slightly see her parents sitting up in bed, holding each other, and a sorrowful cry can be heard from both. The sound of the cry is almost unnatural and comes from the inner depths of their souls in their tragic loss.

Without wanting to startle her parents, Mary does not turn the light on and whispers in Gabriel's ear, "What should I do?"

Gabriel then quietly takes her hand, walks her over to a chair that is located next to the moonlit window, and has her sit down. Gabriel now slowly walks over to the bedside where Tom and Pamela are and says, "I don't mean to scare you, but I must talk to you."

Slightly startled, they see it is Gabriel that is standing next to the bed. They ask him to sit down on the bed with them, and then they hug him as lovingly as if he was their own son.

Tom then says, "Gabriel, what are you doing here? You should be home in bed. I am sorry that I left you at the hospital, as my only thought was to get Pamela home."

Gabriel responds, saying, "It is okay. I had some unfinished business to do anyway." Gabriel then says, "I have a big surprise for you, and when you see the surprise, I want to be sure that you don't freak out or get crazy."

Tom says, "Gabe, in our present state of mind, I don't think this is the time for any great surprises."

Gabriel now motions to Mary, and she stands and walks over to the bedside. As her parents are sitting on the bed in the moonlit room, they can see a shadowy image of a person standing there. However, they are not sure who this person could be.

Mary then says, with her voice softly cracking, "Mom, Dad, it is me."

Tom and Pamela, trying to process what is

going on, say, "It is who?"

She then sits down on the bed next to them, begins to cry, and says, "It is me, Mary."

Tom says, "How can this be?"

As they hug, great emotions and crying can be heard, and it is truly a scene that can only be imagined. Only by the grace of God has this miracle occurred and reunited Tom, Pamela, and Mary again as a loving family. Tom now puts his arm around Gabriel, pulls him in, and all four hug and cry with great loving and happiness.

CHAPTER 8

It is the next morning, and the hospital calls the Hart household. As Pamela answers the phone, she receives instructions to come to the hospital at 11:00 a.m. with Mary and Gabriel. Pamela agrees, they finish breakfast, and all get dressed in preparation to leave for the hospital. Pamela then calls Gabriel's house, and Sarah answers the phone.

Sarah asks Pamela, "What happened last night? It is on every television and radio station about the accident and that six students and the limousine driver are in the hospital in serious condition. Is Mary one of the kids?"

Pamela says that Mary was in the accident but is home and now in good condition.

Sarah says, "What do you mean NOW in good condition?"

Pamela says, "There is something Tom and I want to tell you and Joseph in person but not over the phone. Can you come over for dinner tonight, say around 6:00 p.m.?"

Sarah says that they will be there and is puzzled about what is going on. Before they hang up, Pamela says that they have an appointment at the hospital, and she requests that Gabriel go with them, saying that they will pick him up around 10:30 a.m.

Sarah says, "That will be fine, and Gabriel will be ready."

At 10:30 a.m., Gabriel is picked up, and on their short trip to the hospital, hardly a word is spoken. When they arrive at the hospital, they go the emergency room and tell the nurse about their 11:00 a.m. appointment. The nurse smiles and then looks at Mary with a look of wonderment on her face. Within five minutes, three doctors in white medical coats and two men in suits approach them and ask them to accompany them. It is only a short walk, and they enter the hospital director's office and ask them to be seated.

As all are waiting, the hospital director, Dr. Nelson, then enters the room, smiles, introduces himself, and shakes hands with Tom, Pamela, and then Gabriel. He then walks up to Mary and gives her a hug and says, "How are you feeling this morning?"

Mary smiles at him and says, "I feel just fine."

Dr. Nelson walks over to his desk, sits down, and says, "I must talk to you all this morning, of course, about what happened last night."

Mary immediately interjects and asks, "How are my friends doing?"

Dr. Nelson says, "They are in critical condition. However, by the grace of God, they are all expected to recover. A couple of kids will have to attend physical therapy sessions, but we are hopeful that they will have no permanent injuries. The limousine driver is still in critical condition, though, and we are not sure of his outcome at this point."

Dr. Nelson then says, "We want to discuss the events that took place last night as Mary entered the hospital." He introduces the attending doctors who assisted Mary and asks Dr. Leas, who is the head emergency doctor, to go over the night's procedures.

Dr. Leas takes them through the medical procedures they used to try to keep Mary alive, telling them, "Every bone in her body was broken, and she was unconscious. In fact, Mary's body had shut down, and only a faint signal from the EEG, or electroencephalogram, which is a test that measures and records the electrical activity of your brain, was the reason we had to wait to declare Mary dead. Finally, there was no more electrical impulse from the EEG, and we pronounced Mary dead. That is when I came to you, Mr. Hart, and gave you the bad news."

Tom asks, "But Dr. Leas, how can this possibly happen? Not only was she declared dead with no EEG activity, every bone in her body was broken. How can she be walking and talking with us now? It doesn't make any sense."

Dr. Leas replies, "It absolutely makes no sense. Sometimes we can get a false EEG reading, but her badly damaged skeletal frame makes it impossible for this to have happened. Not only did I declare Mary's body severely damaged with no positive EEG reading, this was also confirmed by the other two doctors here with me today. It is a medical mystery, and I have no answers for you."

For the next five seconds, everyone in the room glances at each other, and not a word is spoken. Dr. Leas looks over at Gabriel, who is sitting quietly in his seat, and says, "Why did you decide to go down to the morgue last night?"

Gabriel replies, "I could not believe that Mary was gone and had an impulse to see her one more time."

Dr. Leas says, "But how did you know which autopsy unit she was in? And once you saw Mary supposedly dead, what happened next?"

Gabriel then explains the events that took place, but he does not tell them that he prayed for Mary and that his tears of blood touched her face. He simply states that as he held her hand, he could feel a slight twitch, and from then on, she just awakened on her own. Everyone in the room stares at Gabriel with questionable looks on their faces, trying to figure out what really did happen.

Tom speaks up and says, "If it wasn't for Gabriel going to Mary, she would probably be dead right now. Is that correct, Dr. Leas?"

The doctor replies that Mary would have died, as her body could not have sustained the cold refrigerated unit she was in. Dr. Nelson then requests that Mary come back to the hospital the following week for an extensive physical examination at no cost to them. Tom and Pamela both agree that it is a good idea, just to make sure Mary is in good overall health.

As they stand and shake hands, Dr. Nelson thanks them for coming to the hospital and says, "If there is anything that we can do for Mary, please let me know." They then leave the hospital and head home.

As they pull up to their driveway, they can see numerous news people, television cameras, and vans all awaiting their arrival. Their car is immediately surrounded, and they can see from inside the car much shoving and commotion. They get out of the car, and Tom respectfully asks everyone to be orderly, telling them he will answer all of their questions.

Pamela, Mary, and Gabriel enter the house, and for the next fifteen minutes, Tom answers questions to the best of his ability. Once the last question is answered, the news crews depart, and Tom enters the house. After discussing with Pamela what happened outside, he notices that Gabriel is not there. Pamela states that Gabriel went home about ten minutes ago, slipping out the back door.

At dinner that night at the Hart's home, after finishing the main course and beginning to have their lemon pie dessert, Sarah asks Pamela, "What really did happen last night? The only information we have is what the television news stations report, and Gabe, you have said nothing to us about what happened."

Pamela then tells the entire story, about how Mary was declared dead and, later, how Gabriel brought Mary back home from the hospital. As everyone sits around the dinner table, the room grows quiet, and all eyes focus on Gabriel. Gabriel looks around the table and sees that everyone is waiting for him to speak.

Mary, who sits next to Gabriel, takes his hand in hers and says, "Please, Gabriel, tell us what really happened. You forget that I was with you when you brought the school principal back to life. Please, tell us the true story of what is really happening. You are amongst family and truly good friends. We all love you, and what you tell us will never leave this table, I promise." Gabriel just sits in his seat, looking down at his dessert plate, and still does not speak.

Then Gabriel's mother, Sarah, speaks up and says, "Your father and I have something to tell you, Gabe, as we have never said a word to you about this." She then tells Gabriel about his baptism, how a Red Cross appeared on his forehead when the holy water touched his head, and that Pastor Maragelis believed that it was a sign from God. "Your father and I knew from that time that you were special, but we never mentioned it to you, as we did not want it to alter your life in any way. Gabriel, for some reason that we do not know or understand, you have been chosen by God to be one of His Disciples. In what capacity is still yet to be seen. However, you saved the school principal and now you were present with Mary's miraculous recovery. Can you please share with us what is really happening?"

Gabriel finally relents and tells the entire story of how he brought Mary back to life, how he prayed, placed his hands on Mary, and how his tears gently fell upon her face. "It is like I go into a trance and have an out-of-body experience, and I could actually see myself from a distance, standing over Mary's body. Right after that is when I believe Mary came back to life. I cannot explain it, however. I am just following what my heart and mind have instructed me to do." Gabriel places his hands over his face and begins to cry.

Mary hugs Gabriel and says, "Thank you, as you have saved my life," and begins to cry herself. All of the parents now have tears in their eyes, knowing that Gabriel saved Mary's life and that he has been truly chosen by God to be an earthly Disciple and Savior.

Over the next few weeks, all of the kids involved in the accident are released from the hospital. Three kids, including Chad, receive some physical therapy but eventually fully recover. The limousine driver also recovers but is in jail with an arraignment soon to take place. It is truly a miracle that none of the occupants in the limousine were killed or permanently disabled. However, Mary had actually died.

CHAPTER 9

The next three years seem to fly by, and both families remain in close friendship. Gabriel and Mary complete their senior year at Grant High School, and both families attend the graduation ceremony. The summer plans for Mary are for her to work at the local hospital as a training nurse's aide and then to attend the local university to get a four-year degree and become an RN and then a nurse practitioner. However, plans for Gabriel are different for a young man of only 18 years of age.

Gabriel has earned his Eagle Scout (the highest rank attainable in the Boy Scout program) and is interested in helping people who are in dire straits, who are in poverty and life-threatening situations. And the only way he can pursue his passion is by becoming a Peace Corps volunteer, though typically, most volunteers are college graduates. Gabriel has been pursuing this since the beginning of his junior year and has completed all of the basic requirements to become a volunteer. He has taken his SATs at the end of his junior year and scored in the upper one percent of the nation, and being an Eagle Scout has entitled him to join the Peace Corps without a college degree. His plans are to work towards his college degree while on assignment, which is paid by a special grant through the federal government.

Gabriel has only a couple of days to get all of his affairs in order and pack for his departure, and it is a bittersweet time for him. He is really excited to depart for Rwanda, but he is sad at the thought of leaving his parents, friends, and, of course, Mary. He will be on a two-year assignment and will not be returning back home until the assignment is over.

Sarah asks Gabriel if he would like to go out for dinner the night prior to his departure, and he replies that he would rather stay at home and invite Mary and her parents over, since they are like family. At dinner that final evening, everyone sits at the dinner table, prepared to enjoy the feast that Sarah has made. She is serving all of Gabriel's favorites: breaded pork chops, mashed potatoes, milk gravy, cucumber salad, rutabaga, rolls, and lemon pie for dessert.

As they prepare to indulge in the delicious dinner, Joseph, Gabriel's father, asks everyone to join hands and create a circle of energy for a special prayer. "Dear Heavenly Father, thank You for this wonderful meal that Sarah has prepared for us. Thank You for watching over all of us, as we are truly blessed with good health, good friends, and loving families. Christ, we ask in Your name that You please watch over Gabriel as he begins his life journey and that You protect and guide him. Christ, we know that Gabriel has been chosen by You to be a special messenger and Disciple and that his journey shall lead him into new and adventuresome places. We know that the will of God will never take him where the grace of God will not protect him. In Jesus' name, I pray. Amen."

As they all toast with their glasses and then enjoy the delicious dinner, there is much laughter and reminiscing of the many trips and great times that the two families have shared over the years.

When the last bite of the lemon pie is finished, Gabriel says, "I must share my thoughts with everyone. Mom and Dad, I can't begin to express to you how much I love you for raising me and setting a wonderful example for me to follow and for also raising me as a Christian and showing and teaching me the true love and power of Jesus Christ."

Gabriel begins to cry, as do Joseph and Sarah, as there is a love between a father, mother, and son that can't be matched. Gabriel wipes his eyes and says to Tom and Pamela, "Thank you for being like my surrogate parents. I love you as if you were my own family, and in my heart, you are."

He then looks at Mary, who is seated next to

him, and takes her hand in his. With his eyes still filled with tears, he says, "Mary, you have been my best friend and confidant ever since the first day we met and sat together in kindergarten. I honestly feel in my heart that Christ has brought us together and has a plan for us to follow. Mary, I love you and have always loved you."

Mary stands up, still holding Gabriel's hand, and with her big, blue, tear-filled eyes, she looks directly into Gabriel's eyes and says, "Gabriel, ever since that day in kindergarten on the school grounds when you came to my rescue from the school bully, I knew that I loved you and have always known in my heart that we would someday share our lives together. Gabriel, I too love you with all my heart and pray that someday we will truly be together."

Gabriel stands, and they hug, and everyone has tear-filled eyes. Joseph now stands up and says, "This is truly a wonderful time. Mary, we love you as if you were our own daughter, and someday in the future, our families will unite, and we all couldn't be happier. God has certainly smiled down upon us, and we are forever thankful for His blessings."

CHAPTER 10

The next morning, Joseph, Sarah, Gabriel, and Mary are at the airport gate, awaiting Gabriel's departure. There is not much conversation, as everyone has an empty feeling in their stomach and saddened by Gabriel's departure. Finally, the airline announces the last call for his flight, which is departing for Miami. With teary eyes, Gabriel hugs his mother and then his father and they tell him how proud they are of him and to be sure to call, if he can, when he reaches his final destination.

He then turns and looks at Mary, who has a very difficult time containing her emotions. Gabriel hugs Mary and tells her that he loves her and that he will miss her. Mary cannot even look at Gabriel, as she is truly depressed that Gabriel is leaving her. They begin to kiss, but it is soon broken off, as Mary begins to weep and can no longer hold back her true emotions.

Mary, in a weak voice, says, "I love you, Gabriel, and I will be here for you when you come back home."

They kiss again, and Gabriel picks up his carry-on duffle bag and departs for the airplane without looking back, as it is too emotional for him to leave the three most important people in his life. Gabriel then boards the plane, goes to his seat, and gets settled in for the first leg of his flight, which is to Miami, Florida. During the flight, Gabriel again reads about his final destination, Rwanda. Gabriel has picked Rwanda because it is a small Eastern African nation that experienced genocide in the 1990s, and many of its current population are poor, in need of much medical attention, and the victims of diseases such as cholera and dysentery.

As Gabriel arrives at the Miami airport, he transfers planes and takes seat number #33C on Flight #23. The plane departs Miami for a long flight of approximately fifteen hours to Rwanda. However, with the reading materials that he has brought with him and the movies supplied by the airlines, the first six hours go as well as can be expected. He also becomes acquainted with his flight neighbor, Jay, who is seated next to him, and they talk about their families and why they are going to Rwanda. In their conversations, Gabriel realizes that Jay is a Christian with a strong belief in Jesus. As the flight continues, both men take power naps, a difficult thing to do with the constant roar of the engines and passengers walking up and down the aisles to exercise their legs and take a bathroom break.

From one of these naps, Gabriel is awakened

by the sound of thunder. As he looks out of his window, he can see in the black sky lightning that makes all the fireworks shows that he has ever seen appear pale in comparison. The lightning show goes on for around fifteen minutes and is certainly a sight to behold.

Suddenly, a bolt of lightning strikes the right jet engine and within an instant, the airplane drops about a thousand feet in elevation. Gabriel's stomach feels like it is on the ceiling. Then the airplane engines make a racing sound, and the plane rocks back and forth as if dangling on a string.

Everyone on the plane screams and cries as the plane continues its downward descent, and it appears out of control. Looks of terror spread across passengers' faces, and some passengers gasp for breath. Oxygen masks drop from consoles above the passengers' heads as people frantically place them over their faces and take deep breaths.

Gabriel, too, is frightened; he has never experienced an emergency situation such as this. As the plane continues its rapid descent, the passengers sit back in their seats and squeeze their armrests. Gabriel stands and looks around the airplane, and it is as if everything is happening in slow motion. He can no longer hear the engines. It is completely silent, and the entire scene seems surreal.

He sits back down, buckles his seat belt, and says to himself, "Is this how it is going to end? I haven't had a chance in life to work for Christ, to be His disciple, to spread His loving word, to help others in need, and to be married to Mary and have children of my own."

Gabriel now bows his head and begins to pray to God, expressing his love for Him. "Christ, Thy Heavenly Father, I love You with all of my heart and soul. If this is my time to depart from this earth, then I accept it openly and without any reservations. I want to thank You for being my Lord and Master and for all that You have bestowed upon me in my lifetime. Thank You for my loving family and friends and for being with me in spirit every step of the way. Thank You for making me the person that I have become and for the special blessing of being a healer for Mr. Kleiner and Mary, whom I love very much. I love You, God, and believe that Jesus is my Savior and ask that You please take me into Heaven so that I may have everlasting life with You. In Jesus' name, I pray." Then, in an instant, there is no more consciousness. However, it is as if Gabriel has been placed inside an invisible bubble and is being protected.

Within one hour, the news of the airplane crash is on every television and radio station in the

United States and then eventually around the world.

Joseph is outside, working in the yard, and Sarah is in the kitchen preparing an early afternoon snack when the telephone rings. It is Pamela, who, with a shaky voice, tells Sarah to turn on the television. Sarah does so, and there, on the news, is the report about how American Airlines Flight #23 from Miami to Rwanda has gone off the radar and is presumed down in the Atlantic Ocean.

Sarah, listening to the news commentator, drops the phone and runs out to Joseph, who is just walking out of the garage with a rake in his hand. Joseph sees that Sarah is crying and quickly walks up to her, saying, "What's wrong? Why are you crying?"

Sarah drops to her knees, and Joseph grabs her to keep her from completely falling to the ground. With a sorrowful cry, Sarah tells Joseph that Gabriel's flight has crashed in the ocean.

Joseph, shocked, says, "How do you know this?"

Still crying, Sarah replies, "It is on the television news. It's Flight #23, Gabriel's plane."

Joseph helps Sarah back onto her feet and into the house, and they both sit on the couch and watch the newscast. As they watch and listen to the news commentator, Joseph bows his head and begins to weep. After a couple of minutes, Joseph says to

Sarah that he must go to the airport and speak to American Airlines officials to get any information he can. Without saying a word, Sarah, in a state of shock, walks into their bedroom and lies down on the bed.

After arriving at the airport, Joseph walks up to the American Airlines ticket agent counter and asks to speak to someone regarding Flight #23. The ticket agent looks at Joseph with dismay and directs him to the administrative office of the airlines. As Joseph approaches the office, he sees other people in the hallway who are also there in search of some answers to their questions. After standing and waiting for around five minutes, they are all invited to come into a large conference room and have a seat. While most people sit, Joseph decides to remain standing.

A spokesperson for the airlines enters the room and asks everyone to hold their questions until he has finished. After about five minutes of updating everyone, he opens the conversation for questions. Numerous questions are asked, but the spokesperson does not have any real answers as to what actually caused the accident, where the airplane is, or whether or not the black box (event data recorder) has sent out a signal.

The spokesperson gives them a longitude and

latitude where the plane was last seen on radar but appears to skirt some of the direct questions. Joseph grows irritated by the lack of direct answers and finally speaks up, asking, "In your opinion, what are the chances of survival?"

The spokesperson momentarily pauses and then says with a sorrowful look on his face that considering where the plane went down, the chances for survival are remote. This shocks everyone in the room, and some people begin to cry.

Joseph says, "Then what you are telling us is that there is no hope for anyone to be alive."

The spokesperson replies, "I'm sorry, but it appears that is the case. We have both the Air Force and Navy pilots flying over the area of ocean where we think the plane went down and at this time, there is no sign of survivors or the plane. I am truly sorry for everyone's loss. The last thing we heard from the captain of the airplane is that they were struck by lightning and were descending at a rapid pace. Then we lost contact with the airplane."

Though the others are still in the room crying, Joseph has heard all that he needs to know. He leaves the airport and returns home. He goes to Sarah, who is still lying in bed, and gives her the bad news. Joseph then lies down beside Sarah, and they embrace each other and cry, as this has been a tragic loss in their lives.

CHAPTER 11

A view from above shows the downed airplane amongst the trees and vegetation. The left wing is missing, and the fuselage (main body of the aircraft) has been torn apart. The aircraft has crash-landed on a remote Atlantic island that is not even on the map. The airplane is not on fire, as the experienced captain discharged all of the fuel in the air prior to the crash.

When Gabriel awakens, he is disoriented and unsure of where he is or what has happened. He unbuckles his seat belt and climbs over Jay's body. His first vision is one of horror, as he sees dead bodies throughout the airplane, some lying in the aisles and others still strapped in their seats. In a state of shock, he is shaky, his legs are weak, his face is sweaty, and he is lightheaded. After momentarily pausing, he slowly crawls and steps over dead bodies to where the aircraft has separated and there is light. As he looks outside, it is raining, and he has a difficult time seeing anything other than the trees and vegetation that surround the airplane, though he can see the smoking right engine where the lightning struck.

Gabriel's faculties finally return; he becomes completely cognizant of what has happened and realizes that Christ has spared him from the horrid accident. He bows his head and thanks God for sparing his life and also asks to bless all of the people who were not as lucky. As Gabriel continues to look outside, he can hear the wildlife, with birds singing and parrots squawking, and can hear the raindrops falling upon the trees and vegetation.

As he continues to ponder his situation, he has mixed feelings of loneliness, insecurity, anger, and isolation but also of gratitude, hope, and wonderment as to what life now has in store for him. Gabriel stays in the airplane, which shelters him from the elements, and as the day draws near, the sky turns black, and he realizes that when dawn again arrives, he must remove himself from his immediate environment and seek out civilization. Gabriel begins to cry, falls to sleep, and dreams.

When daybreak comes, Gabriel awakens. At first, he is unaware of where he is. However, in an instant, he is rudely reminded as he looks down the airplane aisle and sees the horror of the lost earthly souls. Gabriel stands and realizes that he is in survivor mode, and his stomach is telling him that he requires food and water. He wanders toward the front of the aircraft, sees the compact kitchen area, and searches for nourishment.

Lucky enough for him, some of the

sandwiches are still enclosed in the refrigerated area, along with packaged peanuts and pretzels and some bottled water, which were undamaged. As Gabriel opens an unwrapped turkey sandwich and unscrews a bottle of water, he knows that he must soon leave the aircraft tomb and venture out in search of civilization. He locates a duffle bag and fills it with food items and bottled water to take with him.

As he steps out of the airplane and onto the ground, the sunlight from above is partially hidden from the trees, and vegetation towers overhead. He walks into the jungle, cautious and observant of his surroundings, as he does not know if there is any dangerous wildlife lurking around the area. After walking in the midst of heavy vegetation and trees for around an hour, he wanders upon a high cliffside and can see for 180 degrees.

From his vantage point, the view of the beach and ocean below and afar is breathtaking. The sky is blue, the sandy beach is almost white, and the ocean is a dark blue in color. As he views both directions, he sees no evidence of any civilization. For the next hour, Gabriel slowly descends, down the slightly rugged and steep terrain, until he finally reaches his destination on the beach near the water's edge.

He turns and looks up to where he began his journey and gets a better perspective of the landscape of the island. As he begins to walk on the beach, the intense sunlight upon his face and clothed body quickly warms him, and he sheds his shirt, leaving him naked from the waist up. He also removes his shoes and socks, which warms his feet. The warmth of the sun feels very good on his bare chest. He sits on the beach, takes a bottle of water out of the duffle bag, takes a sip, and stares out at the ocean. His immediate thought is that he must first find shelter, as the night before was wet, and keeping himself dry and warm should be his top priority. It is still early afternoon, and he realizes that there is still much daylight to find suitable shelter, at least temporarily.

As he continues to walk on the beach for some time, the sand is still warm to his feet, and there is a nice breeze that keeps him from getting too hot. Eventually, he sees in the hillside the appearance of a cave and ventures over to take a look. As he cautiously walks up to the cave opening, he listens and looks very carefully for any sign of wildlife that could possibly be an occupant. He is cautious about entering the cave, as his eyes are not yet accustomed to the darkness, and he is very nervous about what he might encounter.

After standing in front of the cave opening for around five minutes and not hearing a sound, he realizes that he must either leave or take a chance. This is the only sheltered area that he has observed, and he realizes that if he does not take a chance, he might spend the evening wet and cold should another storm come ashore. As Gabriel ventures into the cave, his eyes slowly become accustomed to the darkness, and he can faintly make out the cave walls and floor. After a short walk, he comes to the end of the cave and realizes that this would be a good area for shelter, as there is no evidence of any previous inhabitants.

He walks out of the cave, into the sunlight, and must shade his eyes due to the bright sun glaring down upon him. Gabriel, being an Eagle Scout, has been taught and trained since a young boy to be self-sufficient in situations such as this. He looks for wood to make a fire for the evening, which could possibly become cool. For the remainder of the day, Gabriel gathers enough wood to make a fire and also finds some vegetation and tree limbs to partially enclose the cave opening and to shelter him from the elements. As the day ends, Gabriel is tired and hungry; he has been so involved in his personal project that he has forgotten to eat.

In the twilight, he uses his Eagle Scout skills, rubs two pieces of wood together, and builds a fire on the beach just in front of his new residence. He takes out a tuna fish sandwich and a bottle of water and indulges in both. The sandwich tastes delicious, and the water is very refreshing and quenches his thirst. He wants to eat a second sandwich, but he knows that his food supply is limited and declines his own invitation.

After about an hour of sitting around the fire, Gabriel wanders into his new digs, lies down on the bed of large herbaceous leaves that he has gathered, and quickly falls to sleep from a very exhausting day.

CHAPTER 12

As the next morning arrives, Gabriel is awakened by the sound of ocean waves, which are at high tide. The water is still some distance from the cave; however, now there is only a limited beach area. Gabriel feels emptiness in his stomach and quickly realizes that he must get nourishment and water so as to keep himself strong. After indulging in one of the last sandwiches and a bottle of water, he ventures out onto the beach, looks in both directions, and is unsure what this day will bring. He soon realizes that he must continue to search for any possible inhabitants on the island, as this is his only way to possibly survive a long duration and to possibly get back home to his loved ones.

Gabriel picks up the duffle bag, with the limited supplies and partial clothing, and begins to walk down the beach, looking in all directions for any signs of human inhabitants. After about two hours of walking the beach, the tide has partially receded, allowing a slightly larger beach area where Gabriel can get a better view of the high-peaked terrain.

After another hour of walking, all of a sudden, Gabriel sees in the sky what appears to be gray smoke coming from the top of the hillside and, in his excitement, immediately thinks that there are other people on the island. He puts on his shoes and socks to protect his feet from the ground, rocks, and other earth-covered items that he will have to walk across when climbing back up the high-peaked area. The climb upward is an arduous task, and even though Gabriel is in good physical condition, he becomes somewhat fatigued.

After some time, he reaches the peak, and the land levels off to where he can now walk at a much easier and faster pace. As Gabriel looks up, it is now difficult for him to spot where the smoke is coming from due to the heavy and high vegetation and trees that surround him. He then decides to climb up one of the trees to get a bird's-eye view of the location of the smoke.

As he nears the top of the tree, he has a good view of the terrain below him and can see that the source of the smoke is in close proximity to the tree. He looks down and sees what appears to be a small village of African tribesmen, women, and children all going about their daily routine. Gabriel has mixed emotions, as he is glad to see that the island is inhabited but is unsure if the tribesmen are hostile to strangers invading their privacy and territory.

He continues to watch and sees no evidence of any hostility between the people. What else are his options? He can either continue to stay on his own and possibly never make contact with his loved ones again or introduce himself to the indigenous island inhabitants and see what their reaction will be. After observing from the height of the tree for another five minutes, he makes the decision to walk into the village and take his chances.

Gabriel descends, and when he reaches the ground, he picks up his duffle bag and walks in the direction of the village. Within minutes, he hears the laughter of children playing, though he cannot yet see the village people. As he continues to walk, the village huts come into view, and he can see everyone doing their daily chores.

At first, Gabriel decides to stay out of sight and continues to observe all that is going on. He is very nervous, as making a wrong decision could cost him his life. Just before venturing into the village, he bows his head and prays to God that he might be protected from any violence that he might encounter. He then takes a deep breath and slowly approaches the village entrance.

Within moments, one of the children sees Gabriel, extends his arm outward, points at him, and screams out. Immediately, the entire village becomes aware of his presence, and all of the village people run up to within twenty feet of Gabriel and just stand there looking at him. Gabriel gets down on one knee, bows his head, and looks up so as to show the people respect and that he means them no harm. What appears to be the village leader then walks toward Gabriel with spear raised. The leader says nothing and just stares at Gabriel.

Not sure what he is to do, Gabriel extends his right hand in a friendly gesture in hopes that the village leader will understand his meaning. With a stern look on his face, the village leader walks up to within two feet of Gabriel, stares down at him, looks him in the eye, and then, in an instant, a smile appears on his face.

The village leader grabs Gabriel's hand in a friendly manner and tries to communicate in his native language. Gabriel, of course, has no clue as to what the village leader is saying, only that he appears to be friendly, and he smiles back. Gabriel pats the man on the back in a friendly manner, and they walk towards the center of the village, with all of the tribe's people following.

In the center of the village is a large fire pit used for cooking and is the general meeting area for the village people, with a blazing fire aglow. The two men continue to try and communicate with gestures rather than spoken language, and it is not long until Gabriel and the village leader better understand each other.

As night approaches, Gabriel finds he is rather fatigued, not only from the difficult climb up the peak, but also from the stress of the day. After a bland meal of unidentifiable meats and vegetables, Gabriel is shown a hut where he can sleep and have some privacy.

The next morning arrives, and Gabriel is awakened by the sound of children playing outside his hut. He has no idea of the time of day. He walks out of his hut and over to the fire, where food items are being prepared by the women of the tribe. He looks around and sees that there are no males present in the village, only woman and children going about their daily business.

Gabriel decides to walk around and observe the infrastructure and dynamics of the village. While on his walk, he comes upon one hut that is isolated from the others, with a skull above the doorway entrance. As he stands and stares at the skull, trying to construe its meaning, one of the women quickly approaches him, speaks in her native language, shakes her head, grabs his arm, and attempts to pull him away from the area. Gabriel quickly understands that he is not to be here and follows the woman back towards the campfire.

After some time passes, Gabriel is already

becoming restless. He is not accustomed to just standing around, but where else is he to go? If he ventures away from the village, he can easily get lost, and if he stays in the village, he will soon become bored.

Another hour passes, and all of the males return with the day's hunt and specific plants and roots with which to contribute to the day's meal. The men skin the dead animal and clean the carcass, and the women prepare the plants and roots and place the items in dried handmade clay pots filled with boiling water that sit over the fire. A short time later, the animal carcass is placed over the fire on a manually operated, handmade rotisserie.

The village leader comes over to Gabriel, and they continue to try and communicate and exchange ideas. As the day progresses, Gabriel becomes quite hungry. Finally, it is time for everyone to eat the prepared food. Gabriel is given his piece of meat and some boiled plants and roots, and the food actually tastes good, especially since he has not eaten since yesterday.

The day slowly ends, turning to twilight, and the sky is canvassed with beautiful red clouds that only God could paint. Just then, the wife of the village leader comes over to Gabriel and her husband. She weeps and speaks to her husband in her native tongue. The village leader and his wife begin to walk over to the isolated hut with the skull, and all of the village people follow. Once they reach the hut, the village leader and his wife enter, and within a short period of time, much crying can be heard. Gabriel deduces that the person inside the hut must be a family member who is close to death.

As Gabriel approaches the entrance to the hut, one of the men walks up to him and grabs his arm to stop him from entering, as the local custom is that only the family can be present when a loved one is near death. Gabriel looks at the man, stares him in the eye, and then enters the hut. He enters the hut and sees that it is somewhat illuminated by flickering firelight from a torch. Both the village leader and his wife are on their knees, on both sides of a small figure lying on a mat, and holding the figure's hands. As Gabriel walks up, he can see that the figure is a young boy of around five years of age and that he is very still and appears to be unconscious.

Gabriel touches the boy's forehead, and he is cold and lifeless. As the boy's parents look up at Gabriel, he gets down on both knees beside the boy, takes the boy's hand in his left hand, and places his right hand on the boy's chest, around the heart area. Gabriel now bows his head and begins to pray to God, asking for permission to save this young child.

As Gabriel is in deep meditation, a Red Cross appears on his forehead, and tears of blood drop gently onto the boy's face.

Within an instant, the fire from the torch flickers from a strong wind as Gabriel stays very quiet over the body. Within a short period of time, the boy makes a groaning sound, his eyes slowly open, he gently smiles at his parents, and he says to them in his native tongue, "I saw a light, and it called to me. I walked over to the light, and I saw a man in white clothing with a gentle, kind smile on his face, and he told me to walk through the light. That is all I can remember."

The boy's parents hug the child. They cry with an abundance of tears, knowing that Gabriel has returned their son to life. The boy sits up and says to his parents, "I'm hungry." Both the village leader and his wife grab and kiss Gabriel's hands and realize the miracle that he has just performed. They all walk out of the hut, and the village people see that the young boy has been healed, and there is much cheer and happiness from all.

As Gabriel follows them out of the hut, the village people surround him, wanting to touch him. Gabriel says to himself, "Thank you, God, for healing this young boy and bringing happiness back to this family."

CHAPTER 13

It is now some months later, and Gabriel has indoctrinated himself within the tribe to the point where he now assists them in all of the duties. He has helped the village people improve their village in many different ways, such as by building a water reservoir, constructing an in-ground natural cooler to help preserve their food for many days rather than having to hunt and gather on a daily basis, and constructing a drainage system so that when the heavy rains come, they will not flood the village.

However, even though Gabriel has been keeping busy, he is saddened that he cannot be with his family and Mary. Gabriel realizes that this is God's plan for him, as he is actually performing duties similar to what he would have been doing had he arrived at his original destination.

Time continues on, and it has now been six years since Gabriel crash-landed on the island. His hair is long, and he has a shaggy beard that he periodically trims with a spearhead. He has greatly improved the village and is considered to be of equal importance and prestige as the village leader. Gabriel often looks out over the cliff side at the ocean in hopes that he might see a ship or visitors to the island so he can again get back to civilization. He actually loves the village people, who have become his surrogate family, and they, in turn, love and respect him as one of their own.

One particular early summer morning, Gabriel feels adventuresome and decides to hike down the high-peaked terrain, onto the beach, and back towards the crashed aircraft. As Gabriel walks on the beach, many thoughts run through his head, including memories of his mom and dad, growing up, Mary, and the many dinners and trips that the two families shared together. Despite being about wonderful times that he will always remember, the thoughts also make him sad and bring tears to his eyes because they make him yearn to again be back home.

After walking for hours on the beach, he sees the cave that he previously used for shelter, which seems now so long ago. Gabriel comes up to the cave opening and, without thinking, walks right into the darkened cave. As he sits down and looks out onto the ocean, he remembers back when he temporarily called this home and has flashbacks of that particular moment in time. Still sitting on the ground, looking out at the ocean, he has a sense that he is not alone, that there is a presence with him in the cave. He nervously turns his head and sees nothing. Within a short period of time, however, he again feels uneasy. As Gabriel stares towards the back of the cave, his eyes slowly grow accustomed to the lack of light. He stands up, slowly walks towards the back of the cave, and then immediately stops.

As he looks more intensely into the darkness, he can barely see two white circular objects staring right at him. Gabriel freezes where he stands, as the white objects slowly get larger and then rapidly approach him. He then hears a grunting sound, and within an instant, right in front of him is a large silverback gorilla.

Gabriel is frozen with fear. He cannot take his eyes off this large creature, and his mind is blank with terror. The gorilla limps up to within two feet of Gabriel and puts its face so close that Gabriel can actually feel the warmth of the air from the gorilla's nostrils and can smell its breath. Gabriel does not move, and the first thought that enters his mind is not one of fear, but that of Jesus.

Standing there, face to face with this great silverback, Gabriel bows his head. He does not make eye contact with the creature, but shows submission. He calmly and slowly raises his right hand and places it on the right cheek of the large animal. Within a couple of seconds, though it seems like forever to Gabriel, the silverback, still staring at him, squats down. At the same time, the gorilla places its large hand on Gabriel's right cheek.

Gabriel looks up so the two are eye to eye again. He can see tears in the animal's eyes and can sense that this great creature has been injured and is in pain. With a sense of calmness, Gabriel asks God to grant him the power to heal this creature. At that moment, a glowing Red Cross appears on Gabriel's forehead and slightly illuminates the darkened cave.

The large silverback's eyes are immediately drawn to the illuminated Red Cross, and a look of bewilderment is expressed on his face. Just then, the great creature cries out, which confirms Gabriel's thought that the gorilla is experiencing great pain. Gabriel now wipes his own tears from his eyes and rubs the fluid on the gorilla's right cheek. In an instant, there is immediate silence from the great creature. The gorilla moves back away from Gabriel without a limp in its step and walks towards the cave opening. As the gorilla leaves the cave, it looks back at Gabriel with almost a human look of appreciation and ventures up the cliff side and out of sight.

Gabriel, still at the cave entrance, thanks God for protecting him. He is amazingly at ease at what has just transpired. Gabriel walks down to the beach, which is at low tide, and tries to remember and recognize the location of the high-peaked area that he originally descended after the plane crash. As he thinks he has a pretty good idea of the approximate location, he begins to climb up the steep terrain. However, it seems that the climb is not as arduous as previously remembered due to the fact that he has become accustomed to the topography of the area.

Upon reaching the top of the peak, Gabriel ventures into the heavily vegetated and tree populated area in search of the airplane. After some time of walking through the area, the winds begin to pick up, and the sky turns a dark gray in color. Gabriel cannot see the sky through the thick foliage, but with the winds and sudden drop in temperature, he realizes that a storm is headed his way and that he must find shelter fast, as this is not just any storm but a large tropical storm.

Gabriel runs through the thick vegetation and trees, and to the right, he sees the aircraft. Rain soaked and out of breath, he just makes it to the airplane and climbs inside. As he sits on the floor of the aircraft, he puts his head back against a wall, closes his eyes, and realizes that he is lucky to have made it to shelter.

The entire area is now dark with streaks of light from the flashing lightning, and loud booms of thunder fill the air. As Gabriel sits there, still catching his breath, he turns his head and looks down the darkened aisle of the airplane to see a graveyard of partially clothed skeletons periodically lit with the lightning. It is truly a terrifying sight to see, and it sends chills up Gabriel's spine and makes the hair on his body stand on end.

Gabriel is still both physically and mentally exhausted from the encounter with the silverback and then running for shelter from the storm, and this vision of the past of the plane crash that had taken so many innocent lives nearly overcomes him. He now covers his face with his hands and begins to break down and weep, falling into a temporary depression.

Very quickly, though, his depression turns to anger, and he says to God, "How could you have let this happen? Why didn't you just let me die with the other passengers? I don't understand why I am being tested. What do I have to do to prove that I love and believe in you? You have blessed me with this great gift of healing power, but how can I best serve you on this almost deserted island? I am so lonely. I miss my loved ones back home, and I now feel like I want to die."

Gabriel continues to cry until, exhausted from expressing all of his emotions, he shuts his eyes, leans back against the wall of the airplane, and falls to sleep. As Gabriel sleeps, he dreams of his family, his childhood, and Mary, and it is almost like his entire life flashes before him in a dream state. Outside, the landscape is dark, lightning strikes in the air, and horizontal rain and high winds continue to shake the airplane.

CHAPTER 14

It is the next morning, and Gabriel is awakened by the sounds of birds chirping and the slight sunlight on his face that reflects off one of the large herbaceous leaves. The storm has blown through the island, and it is again another beautiful day without a cloud in the sky. Gabriel refrains from looking down the aisle of the airplane; he does not want to be reminded of all of the lost lives.

He leaves the plane and heads in the direction opposite to the one he had originally taken, to the other side of the island. As he hikes, he feels that if he wants to get home, he must be more diligent in his search endeavors. While walking through the heavy landscape, he realizes that he must again get down to the beach area where he can visually analyze where he is headed. After descending the semi-steep terrain, he finally reaches the beach area and looks behind him to see where he has been. He walks on the beach for some time until he hears, at the base of the cliff side, a waterfall. He walks over, looks down from the top of the waterfall, and sees where the water pools. It is a beautiful sight, one that might be seen in a vacation tourist magazine.

After a few minutes of viewing the beautiful

scenery, he decides to hike down the side of the waterfall to get a better idea of what is really there. After about fifteen minutes of descending, he comes upon the pool of water, and it is as clear as anything he has ever seen. Towards the rear of the pond, the water is still, and when Gabriel looks into the water, he can see his reflection, and his own image is almost startling to him. He sees that he has lost some weight, is almost skinny, and he sees his bearded face and long hair. He thinks to himself that he looks like one of the street people who hold up signs on the corner that read "Homeless Christian – Any spare change would help." But what else would he look like? He has been away from civilization for over six years.

As Gabriel continues to stare into the pond, he feels the need to bathe, so he strips down and slowly walks into the water. He enters the water and is pleasantly surprised that the water is very warm and not cold as he expected. He thinks to himself that there must be a hot spring close by, as the water is probably around 90 degrees. He floats on his back in the water, closes his eyes, and for the first time in years, is completely relaxed.

As he continues to relax in the water, the sun peeks over the hillside, and the heat of the sun on his face and chest, along with the warmth of the water, almost puts Gabriel into a dream state. In fact, as he relaxes completely, he dreams of home, family, and, of course, Mary.

After around fifteen minutes of relaxation, he decides to swim underwater to see how deep the pond might be. He submerges and views the sub-terrain, spotting an area towards the bottom that looks like it might lead to a cave opening. Gabriel comes up for air, but the opening has caught his attention, and being naturally curious, he decides to take another look.

Gabriel first gets out of the water and puts on his pants, shirt, and shoes to protect himself from any possible injury should he scrape up against the underwater rock wall. He takes another deep breath, descends, and heads for the cave-like opening. As he swims into the opening, he can see light above him and swims as fast as he can towards the light. He quickly reaches the lighted area, swims straight up, and in an instant, his head is above water, and he gasps for air. As he treads water, he looks around the inside of the cave, which is brightly lit with glowing stalactites and stalagmites.

The stalactites that hang from the ceiling and the stalagmites coming up from the ground offer a beautiful array of colors, and the glow is so bright that it appears that one would be in a well-lit room.

Gabriel swims over to the edge of a low embankment, turns, and looks behind him to see where he has been.

The water in the cave is now hot, at approximately 105 degrees, and steam is rising off the water. As Gabriel gets out of the water and onto dry land, he is in awe of the beautiful colors and surreal appearance of the cave. It is like a natural sauna. With all of the steam and warmth of the cave, however, it is a little difficult to breathe. After viewing the beautiful colors for a few more moments, Gabriel begins to slowly walk towards the other end of the large cave; carefully watching his step, as to fall on any of the stalagmites would surely cause him injury.

As Gabriel continues to walk around all of the stalagmites, he observes all of the different natural rock and mineral formations and glowing light show. However, in an instant, Gabriel loses his footing on one of the rocks, falls against one of the sharp mineral structures, and cuts his right side just under the rib cage. As he grabs the injured area, he can see blood staining through his shirt and is in immediate pain and agony.

He lifts himself up from the rock, takes off his shirt and sees that he is badly bleeding. He walks over to a nearby small pool of water, uses his shirt as a cloth, dips the shirt into the water, and begins to wash the blood off the injured area. As he is in agony, he then applies pressure to the area with hopes of slowing down the blood flow. He starts to become lightheaded, as the pain from the injury has now become excruciating. He washes the area, uses his shirt as a tourniquet, and then sits down on the ground to apply pressure to the injured area.

After about ten minutes, the bleeding finally stops, though the wound is still very painful. Gabriel lies back on the ground, holding the injury. Still somewhat dizzy, he closes his eyes and falls into a light slumber. As he sleeps, he has flashbacks of the plane crash, the past six years of living with his surrogate family, and all that he taught them and in turn all that they also taught him, not only about their own culture but also about their beliefs, no matter how primitive. Even though they had never heard of Jesus, they still believed in a supreme being that exists in the sky, which directs their lives in a moral, ethical, and spiritual manner.

Gabriel awakens after a period of time, opens his eyes, and at first is unaware of where he is. As his eyes come into focus, he can again see the brightly colored stalactites above him, and he just continues to stare at the beautiful colors. As he slowly sits, up he immediately grabs the wound, which is still in much pain, and realizes that he must get out of the cave and out into the jungle area, where he can breathe some fresh air and possibly find a better tourniquet to administer to his injury.

As Gabriel slowly and painfully walks for another thirty minutes, he feels the temperature change, and the coolness of his surroundings means he is descending farther down in the cave. He continues to walk until he finally sees an opening where sunlight is shining through. He steps out of the cave opening, and the sun is so bright that he must shade his eyes with his hands so as not to be completely blinded. Also, the change in temperature is extreme, as he has just come out of the cave where the temperature was cool, while now the temperature is around 95 degrees.

Gabriel is so exhausted from walking in pain and has so weakened his body that he cannot take another step. He is now very thirsty and knows that if he does not find water soon, he could pass out or even die from dehydration. Gabriel drops to the ground and begins to crawl, as he no longer has the strength to walk.

After a couple of minutes, he can go no further and passes out, lying face down on the ground and holding his side with his left hand to protect it.

CHAPTER 15

As Gabriel finally awakens, it is hours later, and the twilight of night has set in, with only a short time before the night sky becomes completely dark. He is lightheaded, his lips are chapped, his face is slightly blistered, and his tongue is swollen from the lack of water and from the exposure of the sun and heat. With all of his strength, he stands up and slowly continues to walk into what direction he does not have a clue, and he does not even care.

After thirty minutes of slowly walking, he hears what appears to be a waterfall. Slowly climbing up to the top of a modest hill, which at first appeared to be much higher, he looks down in the darkness and can barely see a waterfall. He slides his body over the top of the hill and descends, down to the water's edge, where he lies on his stomach, submerging his face in the cool water.

The coolness of the water offers him a sensation of extreme relief, one that he cannot remember ever feeling before. Then he cups his hand and fills his mouth with water. At first, he only drinks a little, as he knows that too much water too fast could damage his kidneys, considering his physical condition. As he slowly ingests the water, he becomes more cognizant of his surroundings, and his lightheadedness slowly dissipates. However, his stomach is telling him that he must also get food, his body needs nourishment so he can again become strong to continue on.

After another five minutes of sitting by the water's edge, he follows the river's embankment, which descends to where, he has no idea. Gabriel, being an Eagle Scout and having been taught by his surrogate family, looks in the dark for certain edible plants and roots that can offer him a temporary solution to his hunger. Finally finding suitable plants and roots, he takes them to the river's edge, washes them, and indulges in what seems to him to be a feast. Even though the roots have little to no flavor, they are still nourishing and will temporarily fill his stomach until tomorrow, when he can search for more food.

As Gabriel finishes his limited supply of roots, his body is still stiff, his injury is still throbbing, and he is exhausted. He looks for shelter, where he can rest, as he knows that he must try and get some REM sleep so he can regain some strength. Eventually, Gabriel finds an area that appears to offer some temporary shelter. He lies on his side in a fetal position, holding his right side with his left hand, as this appears to lessen the pain.

It is a long and restless night, but when he awakens, he feels somewhat refreshed, as he did get some periods of sleep. He lies on the bed of leaves that he prepared for himself, and it is again bright, with the sunlight shining lightly on his face. As he continues to lie still in the fetal position, he is startled by the sound of a wild animal walking that appears to be in close proximity.

As he remains very still, he hears a roar, that of a tiger. Instant fear rushes to his brain, and he does not know if he should stay completely still or try and run over to the pond, which is now some distance away. Gabriel knows that he cannot move quickly with his injury and decides to just stay as still as possible. As he continues to lay still, his heart feels like it is pounding through his chest, and he can actually feel his pulse beat in the temples of his head. Gabriel says to himself, "Is this the way that I am going to die?" He then closes his eyes and begins to pray, "Dear Lord, You have blessed me and kept me safe from harm. I love You and believe in You with all my heart and soul. Please, protect me. I do not believe that You have intended me to die in this fashion, as I feel that I have not yet completed my mission here on earth, my mission to heal the sick and to teach the non-believers and also believers that Jesus Christ is the Son of God, that the way to true everlasting life is through this belief. Thank You, Christ, for being my Savior, and until my last dying breath, I will love, honor, and cherish your name. In Jesus' name, I pray."

Just then, Gabriel opens his eyes and makes eye contact with the tiger, which has spotted him. Gabriel realizes that the smell of blood from his wound has attracted the tiger and that his life is now about to end. As the tiger continues to stare at Gabriel, it races toward him and makes a loud roaring sound.

Gabriel says, "I love You, Christ."

He can see the large animal about to jump on him, but in an instant, the tiger is thrown to the side. Gabriel looks up and sees a large silverback gorilla standing over him. The gorilla pounds his chest, shows his teeth, and makes a loud screaming sound that could easily have been heard for miles.

The tiger again attacks, and the mighty gorilla catches the tiger in mid-air and throws the large cat like it was a doll. The tiger then gets up, looks at the mighty beast, and runs off into the jungle. Then the mighty gorilla looks down at Gabriel, squats down beside him, and just stares at him.

Gabriel, being almost in shock at what has just happened, slowly sits up and stares directly into the gorilla's eyes, not knowing what is now going to happen. Their faces are so close, nearly eye to eye, that Gabriel can smell the silverback's breath.

The great beast lifts his arm and gently strokes Gabriel's right cheek with his hand. Gabriel, in turn, puts his hand on the gorilla's right cheek. The great silverback has tears in his eyes as he looks upon Gabriel. Gabriel realizes this is the great creature that he healed, which is now returning the kindly gesture.

The large gorilla stands up, glances around the immediate area as though making sure it is safe for Gabriel, looks down at him, makes a loud snorting sound, and walks off into the jungle. Gabriel thinks to himself that this great magnificent creature has been chosen to be his protector and temporary earthly angel. God has again answered his prayer, and Gabriel now knows that he is not alone. However, he must continue onward.

As Gabriel continues, his injury is not healing properly. He opens his shirt and sees that it is becoming infected. At day's end, Gabriel finds the beach shoreline, walks down to the water edge, and just stares out at the vast ocean. He is, again, becoming very weak and lightheaded, and he now has a temperature. He walks up to the dry sand, looks upward, and sees in the dark skyline beautiful bright twinkling stars. As he continues to view the beautiful canvassed sky, he closes his eyes and falls to sleep again in the fetal position.

After a restless night with a high temperature and throbbing injury, Gabriel is awakened in the morning by the feeling of movement, and then he hears unfamiliar voices. Lying on his back, he slightly lifts his head, squints, and sees the brightness of the sun and then four men who are carrying him on a stretcher.

One of the men smiles down at Gabriel and says, "Just relax, son. We are here to help you."

At first, Gabriel thinks that he might be delirious due to his high temperature, but then he realizes that this is actually happening. When they reach the lifeboat that has been waiting for them at the shoreline, they lift Gabriel onto the boat. As they push off from the shoreline, Gabriel lifts his head and sees, standing on the beach, the tribal leader and other members of his surrogate family watching with raised spears as if waving good-bye. Just before passing out, Gabriel slowly raises his right arm in a gesture of thanks to his surrogate family, a family that he will never forget, a primitive family that actually saved him and taught him a different way of life.

Back in the distance, at the top of the cliff line where the jungle and heavy vegetation exists is the great silverback. While looking down and out at them, he stands, snorts, puts his hand on his own right cheek, beats on his chest, and then disappears into the jungle.

CHAPTER 16

Gabriel has been unconscious and delirious with a high temperature now for two days. Finally, he is awakened by the movement of the merchant marine ship as, within one hour, they are to encounter a large storm. They are within 100 miles from the Gulf of Guinea, and everyone on the ship is running around strapping everything to the deck and bringing items into the ship's bowels.

As Gabriel sits up in bed, he sees the ship's medic. Then he feels some pain in his right side and sees that it is bandaged.

The ship's medic sees Gabriel, walks over to him, feels his forehead, and says, "Good, your fever is finally down."

Gabriel's first response is to ask, "Where am I, and how did I get here?"

The medic tells Gabriel, "An infrared beacon from the small island where you were located was sent and detected by our ship."

Gabriel then states, "But how could that be, as the only inhabitants on the island are the primitive natives who have no knowledge of any sophisticated sonar devices?"

The medic replies, "It has also been a mystery

to the entire ship crew. We were aware of the island, but to the best of our knowledge, a vessel has not come within miles of the island for many years. We had heard that it was inhabited. However, the island is off limits to all vessels, and if anyone were detected going ashore, the captain could lose his mariner's license and face prosecution. Our captain decided to take a chance and investigate the beacon. When we first arrived on shore, we were met by the island natives, who, in their native tongue and body gestures, told us about a white man who was on the island. They had not seen him for a while, though. So we decided to take our rescue boat and search the shoreline. After about an hour, we saw you lying on the beach, and from there, you know the rest of the story. Just how did you get on the island and how long have you been there?"

Gabriel explains how his plane crashed on the island and how he was the only survivor. That he met the island natives that became his surrogate family, and if it hadn't been for them, he surely would have perished.

The medic then states that he remembers hearing about an airplane that was lost at sea and was never recovered. "My gosh, that was over six years ago!"

Gabriel, hearing how long he has been away,

just puts his head down and thinks of his parents and Mary. Then the medic tells Gabriel that he must look at his wound and replace all of the bandages.

The medic introduces himself as John. He removes the bandages, showing that some of the infection, redness, and swelling of Gabriel's wound has slightly improved. He says to Gabriel, "You are going to have quite a scar." As Gabriel looks down at the wound, he sees that his injury looks like an unorthodox Cross.

John tells Gabriel that they are to encounter a sizeable storm and that it would be best if his chest and waist were strapped to the bed, as the ship could really encounter some rocking and swaying that could possibly throw him around. Gabriel agrees, and a short time later, the storm reaches the ship.

It seems like the storm goes on forever, and it ends up being much worse than anyone expected. There are extremely high winds, and the ship encounters 80-foot swales, which the ship is not designed to handle. In fact, this "Perfect Storm" is classified as a category three hurricane, with winds up to 125 miles per hour.

The ship's siren begins to ring out, informing the crew that the ship's hull has been breached and the ship is beginning to capsize. The ship lists to its side, throwing John across the room. He crawls over to Gabriel's bed, releases the straps from Gabriel, and both men cling to each other for support. They crawl to the door opening, which now faces upward, towards the sky, and not downward, towards the water.

With much force, they are able to slightly open the door. As the door cracks open, the high winds catch it and slam it completely open. Outside, it is dark, and they hear the eerie sound of the wind, see horizontal rain and when they look up, see a swale that dwarfs them, a swale easily around eight stories high. Both men have no time to think, as the ship is going down. They have no choice but to jump and hope for the best.

As they float in the water, it is like they are on a roller coaster. Now riding the swale, it takes them to a height of around 80 feet and then drops them so rapidly they feel like they are to going to the depths of the ocean. They float about forty feet apart, facing each other and helpless to do anything but just ride the swale.

Within a couple of minutes, Gabriel sees a piece of wood decking, torn off by the high winds prior to the ship sinking. The only problem is that he and John are at the peak of the swale and the decking is at the bottom so that, with each swell, it continues to pass just out of reach. This continues for a couple of minutes until Gabriel realizes that his only chance is to swim to the raft in hopes of grabbing onto the wooden structure. He knows that if he cannot reach the raft, they will surely drown. He also realizes that if he doesn't try, he is going to die anyway. As the raft passes by him a couple more times, he tries to time his swim so he can reach the raft the next time it passes. If his timing is off even a couple of seconds, he will not get another chance.

He watches the raft approach, and with all of his strength, he begins to swim. He desperately stretches out his arm, and as luck would have it, he feels the wooden structure hit his hand. As he closes his hand, he can feel a piece of rope that is attached to the structure, and he holds on for dear life.

Gabriel is now towards the back of the structure and is being pulled upward towards the top of the swale. He knows that he cannot let go and that this is his only chance for survival. As he rides the swale a couple of times, he is able to slowly pull himself up and then onto the raft. Now on his stomach, lying on the raft, he looks around in hopes of seeing John, who was in the same general area. At first, he cannot spot him, but with luck, he finally sees him at the top of the swale.

Gabriel knows that the only way he can save John is to tie a piece of the rope around his arm, slide off the raft, and hopefully swim over to him with the raft following. He knows that he must again time his swim. As they pass one another, Gabriel slides off the raft and heads towards John. With all of his might, he reaches out his arm, and the two grab one another, clutching each other until they are eye to eye.

As they embrace, it is like the event is in slow motion, a surreal experience, as if in a dream state. Gabriel positions his body so he can slide onto the raft and then, with all of his strength, pulls John onto the raft. Once the two men are on the raft, Gabriel is exhausted, and both men lie face to face, hugging one another for support and holding on for dear life as the raft continues to ride the swale.

CHAPTER 17

As Gabriel awakens, the first thing he sees is John face down on the raft. He squints upward to see squawking seagulls flying overhead and blue sky and a brightly shining sun behind them. The water and sky are now back to normal; they have survived the hurricane, which is surely a miracle.

Gabriel bows his head and gives thanks to God for saving and protecting John and himself. "Dear Lord, God, our Heavenly Father, thank You for your protection in our time of trouble. Thank You for giving me the strength to survive this life-threatening event, and thank You for being my Lord and Savior. I love and believe in You with all my heart and soul. In Jesus' name, I pray."

Just then, John makes a groaning sound, slightly lifts his head, and sees Gabriel. He slowly sits up and says that he must be dreaming, that to survive the hurricane is unbelievable. How they could survive on such a small wooden raft when the large merchant ship could not is mind boggling to him.

Gabriel looks at John and says that their survival is not just happenchance; a supreme power has been looking out for them. John just stares at Gabriel and says nothing.

Gabriel feels pain in his right side, lifts his shirt,

and sees that his wound is again becoming more infected and swollen. John takes a look at the wound and says that they need to be rescued soon, as the injury can become life threatening from infection. "I hope that we will be rescued soon, as, before the ship capsized, the captain put out an SOS distress signal and any ship in the area will be looking for us. However, they will be looking for a large merchant marine vessel and not a small raft, which is almost impossible to see in this vast ocean. We are like a speck of sand on the beach, and it will take some real luck to be found."

As the day goes on, Gabriel and John reminisce about their lives, and each share stories of where they were born and raised and about their families. As fate would have it, they discover that John was born and raised in the same town as Gabriel and actually attended the same grade school, though he was three years older than Gabriel.

John says, "After I graduated from college, I wanted to become a doctor. However, I felt that I must step up to do my duty to God and country, so I joined the Marine Corps as a medic."

While in the Corps, John assisted many soldiers on the battlefield with minor to life-threatening injuries. Though only 28 years old, John had actually experienced more than most people do in a lifetime. He tells Gabriel that he was blessed to have realized his calling early in life and to have had an experience that changed his life.

Gabriel asks John, "What was that experience?"

John replies, "I can remember it as if it happened yesterday. When I was in grade school, I had some personal issues to get through, as my parents had recently divorced. I was a bully and didn't care about anyone but myself, so I picked on kids in the school. I remember that, one-day, I was in the schoolyard with my friends and walked up to two younger kids. The little girl was eating something, I think it was an apple, and I grabbed it from her. The little girl said something to me, and I pushed her down on the ground. I thought it was pretty funny, and so did my friends. Just then, the little boy that was with her walked right up, looked me straight in the eye, and then placed his hand on my shoulder. When he did that, I recall at that very moment, a warming sensation entered my body, and it is unexplainable to this day. It was as if all of my sadness and anger had been lifted from me, and I knew that I was not alone and that everything was going to be okay."

Gabriel, in his astonishment, realizes that John

was the school bully that Mary and he encountered on the school grounds. That, in his own odd way, John was responsible for Mary and him bonding because of that particular incident. Especially Mary, as she had told Gabriel that it was something that she would never forget, how he had stood up to the big school bully in her defense. Gabriel does not say anything to John, seeing that he has now become a good person, one who thinks of others and wants to help heal those in need through his medical talents.

As the day goes on, the sun continues to shine down on the two, and they have nothing to shade them from the intense heat. That evening, there is an illuminating full moon, and a vast sky full of bright, twinkling stars. They are thankful that they do not have to endure the heat of the sun, but they know that tomorrow will bring more of the same.

Gabriel is now beginning to be in more pain as his wound grows worse, and John is getting quite concerned, as he has no way to administer any degree of medical assistance to Gabriel.

The next morning, the two are awakened by the sounds of seagulls flying overhead, and they have to shade their eyes from the brightly shining sun that greets them. The day is much like the one before, as the two sit on the raft afloat and have no control of their destination. John again looks at

Gabriel's wound and sees that it is still getting worse, and he becomes even more concerned and frustrated with the situation.

Gabriel looks at John, smiles, and says, "Do not worry. I will be okay, as this is just a temporary event in my life that I must endure to become the complete person that God wants me to be."

John then says to Gabriel, "How can you believe that God is looking out for you when you have not seen your family for many years, you were in a plane crash, you were injured while on the island, the rescue ship you were on sank to the bottom of the sea, you are lost afloat on a raft in the middle on the ocean, and your wound is infected and could be life threatening in the next couple of days. I don't understand how God can be looking out for you. It seems to me that God has forgotten about you and there is a black cloud over your head. I have never met anyone in my life that has endured as much as you."

Gabriel replies, "To you, it appears like bad luck, and I can see how it would seem that way from your point of view. However, from my perspective, the events that have transpired in my life are not that of bad luck but are life experiences. God, in His infinite wisdom, wants me to experience all of these events so that I can become the person He wants me to be. It is these difficult struggles that I endure that will make me the person I become once I reach God's definition of spiritual maturity. I am still being tested, and until God is satisfied that I am the person that He wants me to be, I will continue to experience life's struggles. God knew that these events were going to happen. However, it was not something that He planned. He certainly would not have caused other people to die just so I can experience these events. 'Free Will' has taken place, and I must experience whatever happens. At any time, I could die from one of the tragic events, and I truly accept that fact. I am not afraid to die, as I know that Jesus and God are there for me. Jesus died on the cross for us, and He is the way to everlasting life. I believe in Jesus as my Savior, and when the time comes, I welcome my chance to be in Heaven. I do want to be on earth as long as I can, but without Jesus and God in my heart, it would be a lonely and scary place to be. Jesus fills my heart with joy and love, and with this feeling, I know that there is a purpose to life. Everyone has struggles in life, some more challenging than others. It is how you handle these struggles throughout your life that matters. Do you want to take on these struggles with a feeling of emptiness and being alone and hope for the best, or do you want to know that you are not alone and that Jesus is right there with you? I believe that everyone has their own special guardian angel that is always by their side, watching and listening to all their challenges. It is how you handle life's experiences that matters. The Lord does not look at the events in our lives the same as we do. We look at the outward appearance, but the Lord looks at the heart."

John, sitting beside Gabriel on the raft, can see on his face and in his eyes that he truly believes in everything he has just said, and it is a look that John has never seen before, a look of complete love, belief, and calmness, and he is overcome by Gabriel's words. For the first time in his life, he has an understanding of what Gabriel has expressed. He has heard and read these words before, but never in such a personal, sincere, and fulfilling manner.

For the next three days, Gabriel and John are prisoners on the small wooden raft. They are baked by the sun, have no food or water and are dehydrated to the point that they are nearly unconscious. As twilight approaches, Gabriel slowly lifts his head and sees a bright twinkling star above, and he thinks that this star must resemble the guiding light that led the three wise men to Jesus upon His birth. Then, in the distance, he thinks he sees land to the southeast.

Not sure if he is delirious, he lays his head back

down on the raft, lifts his arms up towards the heavens, and with tear-filled eyes and a slight smile on his face, thanks God for His protection and love before again losing consciousness.

Now swimming around the wooden raft are dolphins, and they are actually nudging the raft with their bodies, directing it towards the shoreline. However, Gabriel and John have no conscious awareness of what is occurring.

CHAPTER 18

It is the next morning, and the natives of Guinea-Bissau, where they have landed, are pulling in the wooden raft from the water. Gabriel is unconscious, and John is semi-unconscious and can hear voices that alert his senses. Gabriel is now very sick from his injury and does not move, and John lifts his head to see what is happening. Both men look like boiled lobsters from the intense sun and heat and are dehydrated to the point that their tongues are so swollen they can hardly speak.

As the raft is taken to a dock at the shoreline, they are both lifted from the raft, brought ashore, and placed on locally made bamboo stretchers. They are then transported by an oxen-pulled wagon to the local medical facility that is modest at best. As they are brought into the facility, they are placed on cots and integrated with other patients in an open bay area. The patients' illnesses range from an infected skin rash to some as severe as full-blown AIDS. Actually, it is a morbid setting, as disease is rampant, and often, patients that enter the medical facility for a non-threatening illness end up dying from a non-related disease that they had contracted from other patients.

The local medical care technician walks over to John and begins to ask him questions about how he is feeling. John immediately instructs the technician to look after Gabriel, as he still has not yet moved. As the technician approaches Gabriel, he can see that his shirt has dried and is sticking to the right side of his abdomen, where the injury is located. He tries to lift the shirt off the area and cannot, as it has crusted and must be slowly removed so as not to damage the area even more.

The technician slowly and deliberately removes the shirt, and when he finally views the injury, he has a look of horror on his face. The entire side of Gabriel is so infected that it has also swollen his abdomen. The injury is bright red, swollen, and has seeping puss, which is the actual infection that has taken over his entire right torso area. The technician turns to John, who is lying in the next bed, and states that Gabriel's injury is so bad and infected that he may not be able to be saved.

"I have never seen such a severe infected injury in all my life, and it is beyond my medical ability to stop the infection. This man needs immediate surgery and medicines that we do not have here at our disposal. I am not qualified to perform such a procedure, and even if I was, it is possibly too late to save him. The infection alone is severe, and he has a high temperature, which is the reason he is unconscious. His body, in its own defense, is shutting down, and there is nothing I can do to stop it."

John, in his weakened state, sits up in bed and says that he wants to see for himself how severe the wound is. As he tries to stand up, the technician assists him as his legs are weak and he has limited strength. John looks down on Gabriel's wound, and he too has a look of disbelief, as this injury is as bad as he has ever seen, which includes his time on the battlefield in the Marines. John has viewed and assisted in battle wounds that were so severe that soldiers lost their limbs, but he has never seen an infection such as this.

The technician then says, "We have limited medical supplies here at our facility, as we are a small area, and the local government does not really care about us."

John then asks the technician if there is any way he can contact a hospital with proper doctors and medical staff that Gabriel can be flown to. The technician states that the Royal North Shore Hospital located in Lamin, Guinea, which is approximately one hundred miles south, is the closest medical facility. John then states that he must make contact with that facility to get someone immediately to look after Gabriel.

The technician brings John an ancient walkie-talkie, and he uses it to contact the hospital. John slowly speaks, as it is still difficult for him to talk, and he explains that he and Gabriel are Americans and request the hospital's immediate response. John tells the doctor about Gabriel's injury and severe infection so the correct medicines can be brought. As the conversation is completed, John is told that help is on the way and will arrive in a medical helicopter.

John hands the walkie-talkie over to the technician, who gives them the coordinates of their exact location. Within around 90 minutes, which seem much longer, the helicopter arrives and lands at a clearing close to the medical facility. The doctor and attending nurse run from the helicopter to the facility. They enter the open bay area, and the doctor quickly introduces himself to the medical technician and John as Dr. Yoder.

As Dr. Yoder walks down the open bay area towards Gabriel's bedside, he sees all of the diseased and sick patients. He is disgusted by the sight of the non-cleanliness, with flies everywhere, patients with non-bandaged, open wounds, and some patients with highly contagious diseases that are amongst the small general hospital population.

He approaches Gabriel's bedside and sees an unconscious man with long hair and a beard, whose face is swollen and discolored from the high temperature and burnt from the sunlight. He places his left hand on Gabriel's forehead and, with his right hand, pulls back the sheet that is covering Gabriel's chest. As he uncovers the sheet, one can see the surprised look on his face as he views the infected area. He then looks at John and states the obvious, that the infection is severe to the point that Gabriel is comatose. "Before we can fly him out, we must immediately reduce his temperature, or he will soon surely die."

As Dr. Yoder asks the attending nurse for the correct medicines, she walks around to the other side of the bed, opens the medical kit, and begins to assemble the syringe. After the syringe is prepared, the nurse then takes out clean bottled water and washcloths and begins to clean the wound.

As she is leaning down close to the body, she looks at Gabriel's face, stops what she is doing, has a puzzled look on her face, and then, in an instant, has a blank look of disbelief. The doctor sees what is going on and says, "Are you okay?"

The nurse drops to her knees next to the bed, puts her head down in her hands, and begins to cry almost out of control. Dr. Yoder walks over to the nurse, squats down at eye level with her, puts his hand on her shoulder, and says, "Mary, what is it?"

Mary continues to weep for a short while and then says to Dr. Yoder, "This is Gabriel, my best friend, confidant, and the man I promised my life to. Over six years ago, his airplane was lost at sea, and the plane and passengers were never found. I cannot believe that he is still alive."

Just then, John speaks up and says, "Oh my God! You are the Mary that Gabriel has spoken about. That is simply amazing."

For the next hour, Dr. Yoder and Mary administer to Gabriel the needed medicines and also put ice packs around his body, which they had brought with them on the helicopter. After a period of time, Gabriel's temperature drops a few degrees, and Dr. Yoder indicates that they cannot wait any longer and must get him to the hospital in Lamin, Guinea.

Dr. Yoder, the helicopter pilot, Mary, and the medical technician all assist in getting Gabriel and John aboard the helicopter and then thank the medical technician for his assistance. As the day ends, the medical technician watches the helicopter, with its emergency lights flashing, lift off the ground and fly off into the twilight.

As the helicopter is en route, Mary gives Gabriel a kiss on his cheek and continues to put cold compresses on him in order to keep his body temperature down. She also attends to John, who is also in need of medical assistance.

As the helicopter approaches the hospital landing area, the medical team gets ready to take Gabriel and John to the emergency room. Gabriel is scheduled for immediate surgery, as the infection is so bad that it may be too late to save his life.

CHAPTER 19

It is the next morning, and Gabriel is in the intensive care unit room after a three-hour surgery. Mary is his attending nurse, and she refuses to leave his side. For the entire day, Mary continues to nurse Gabriel, and she becomes more and more concerned the longer he remains in his coma.

Dr. Yoder enters the room, looks at Gabriel, and states that it is not looking promising for him, as the infection has become so severe that it has invaded some vital organs and could possibly affect his heart. He goes on to say that the next couple of hours are critical as to whether Gabriel will survive this massive infection. However, in private, he believes that Gabriel will not live through the night. As night falls, his room is dark, and only the moonlight shines through the window. Mary lets go of Gabriel's hand, stands, takes out a candle from the night bag she has with her, and lights the candle. With the moonlight shining and candle glowing, the room has a peaceful, spiritual ambiance. In harmony, the flickering candlelight and moonlight cast shadows on the walls, and their appearance is almost surreal.

With tear-filled eyes, Mary again takes

Gabriel's hands in hers, bows her head, and begins to pray. "Dear Lord God, our Heavenly Father, of all the prayers that I have said to You in my lifetime, this is truly my most important request of all. Christ, I know that You have been with Gabriel his entire life and most assuredly right now. I know of the special gift that You have bestowed upon him so that he can heal those in need, as he has done in the past, including my life. Christ, please answer my prayer to You. Please, put Your hand on his shoulder so that he may survive and again deliver Your word of everlasting life. I know that Gabriel has many blessings yet to bestow on those in need. I love and believe in You, Christ, and whatever your decision, I will gracefully abide by it. In Jesus' name, I pray."

Mary finishes her prayer, and with tears flowing down her cheeks, she looks at Gabriel. As she is looking at Gabriel, all of a sudden, on the wall appears a shadowy silhouette of angel wings that appears to be slowly moving as if in flight. The motion of the angel wings catches Mary's eye, and she is in awe of what she is witnessing.

At that exact moment, the door to Gabriel's room opens and John slowly enters. He sees that the room is dark, and the flickering candle immediately draws his attention and it takes his eyes a couple of seconds to get accustomed to the shadowy darkness. He walks over to the foot of Gabriel's bed and sees Mary staring at the wall. He looks at the wall and also sees the silhouette of angel wings in motion and cannot believe what he is viewing.

The impact of this sight is so emotional to him that he walks up to the wall, drops to his knees, bows his head, raises his hands, begins to cry, and says, "Christ, I love You. I now know that You exist."

For the next few seconds, the angel wings appear on the wall, and then, in an instant, disappear. As John is still on his knees crying, Mary walks over to him, gets down on one knee, puts her hand on his shoulder, and says, "John, accept the Lord as your Savior, as He is there for you and all of us. Just put your faith in Him, and you will be rewarded with peace and love in your heart and everlasting life." John then hugs Mary and continues to cry, as, for the first time in his life, he now really believes that there is a Savior, and he has a sensation of warmth in his body that goes all the way to his soul.

After a few seconds, they stand and walk over to both sides of Gabriel's bedside. Mary then says to John for them to hold hands, take Gabriel's hands in theirs, and create a circle of energy. As they do this, they bow their heads and begin to say a silent prayer.

A short time later, looking down on Gabriel,

Mary sees his eyes slowly open, and a slight smile appears on his face. As Mary and John continue to look down on Gabriel, their faces glow as if a light is shining. There, on Gabriel's forehead, is an illuminated cross, the same sign that appeared when Gabriel was baptized. Mary now knows that their prayers have been answered and that Gabriel is on his way to recovery.

John wipes his eyes and leaves the room, leaving Mary to be alone at Gabriel's side. Mary is now exhausted, as she has not slept since early yesterday morning, and the intense emotional feelings that she has experienced has drained all of her energy. She lays her body down on the bed beside Gabriel, puts her arm gently over his chest, above the infected area, and leans her head against his. Within a second, she falls asleep. Gabriel knows it is Mary who is embracing him. He glances up at the wall and sees what Mary and John had witnessed, a shadowy silhouette of angel wings in motion. Gabriel says to himself, "Thank you, Lord, for protecting John and me and bringing Mary back in my life." He then closes his tear-filled eyes and falls back to sleep.

CHAPTER 20

It is the next morning. Gabriel awakens and immediately realizes that Mary is not by his side. The sun shines brightly in his room, and he can hear conversations in the hallway outside his room. As he quietly lies in bed, he closes his eyes and goes into deep thought, reflecting on what has transpired in his life the past six years. After about five minutes of recalling all that he has endured, Dr. Yoder enters the room with an attending nurse.

Dr. Yoder walks up to Gabriel's bedside, sees that he is awake, and greets him with a "Good Morning." Gabriel looks at Dr. Yoder, smiles, and says nothing. The doctor pulls back his covers and looks down on Gabriel's abdomen area, where the surgery and infection are located. As he examines Gabriel, he is quite amazed at how rapidly the infected area is healing.

He says, "Someone must have been in your corner, as I honestly had my doubts that you would make it through the night. If you continue to heal at this pace, you could possibly be out of here within a few days, barring any complications. When I first examined you at the Guinea-Bissau medical facility, I honestly did not hold out much hope for you, as your injury and infection were as bad as I have ever witnessed. You must be a strong-willed young man to be able to withstand such infection to your body."

Gabriel's immediate thought is not one of being strong-willed but of having Christ in his life.

After a few more minutes of examination, Dr. Yoder grabs and squeezes Gabriel's hand and says, "The good Lord must have something in store for you." He smiles and then leaves the room.

Gabriel now realizes that Christ is also in the heart of Dr. Yoder. He turns his head on the pillow, closes his eyes, and then falls back to sleep.

For the majority of the day, Gabriel sleeps. He is weak, and his body requires rest, medication, and nourishment from the IVs. Late in the day, he awakens. He realizes that he is beginning to feel stronger and is becoming more cognizant, as his mind is less clouded, which is partly due to the medications he has been taking.

As Gabriel looks out of his window, he hears his bedroom door open, turns his head, and sees that it is Mary. With a sincere smile and tears in her eyes, Mary walks up to Gabriel's bedside, leans down, puts her cheek on his, and gently kisses him. As she kisses him, Gabriel can feel Mary's tears fall gently on his face. Mary turns her head, their noses almost touch, and they are eye to eye.

As Gabriel looks into Mary's tear-filled eyes, he immediately remembers how beautiful her blue eyes are, and it is as if he is looking into blue artesian pools. Gabriel's eyes tear up; he cannot contain himself and begins to cry.

"Mary, I have missed you so much that I cannot even express in words how much I love you."

They kiss again, and tears flow from their eyes. Mary stands up, wipes her eyes, and just stares at Gabriel.

Gabriel takes Mary's hand in his and says, "Mary, I have so many questions to ask," and Mary, in return, says the same to Gabriel.

Mary says, "The first thing we must do is contact your parents, which is going to be quite a conversation."

Gabriel then asks about his parents, in hopes that they are well.

Mary says, "Your parents took the news very hard. Your mother, especially, has not been the same since. She has been in denial and in psychiatric counseling for years now, and your father has had to take care of her. Her diagnosis is that she is in a depressed state. Your father was also depressed. He received some counseling early on and is mentally stronger than your mother. He has continued to keep her from being institutionalized. Their Christian faith has held them together, but it is still very difficult for your mother to let go."

Mary suggests to Gabriel that they wait until he is released from the hospital before his parents are contacted, and he agrees. For the next few days, Mary continues to be at Gabriel's bedside, and John visits frequently, as they are to be released the same day.

On the day of their release from the hospital, Mary employs a stylist to cut Gabriel's hair and shave his beard. Afterwards, Gabriel locates Dr. Yoder and thanks him for all that he has done.

The doctor smiles, shakes Gabriel's hand, and says, "You were a remarkable patient, and I am going to use you as a case study in my upcoming lecture series here at Royal North Shore Hospital."

Gabriel then asks Dr. Yoder if there is any way that medical supplies and assistance can be sent to the small medical facility where he and John were rescued. Dr. Yoder states that it has already been taken care of.

Mary escorts Gabriel and John out of the hospital to her modest apartment, which is located just a few minutes away. John says that he is going to the downtown area of the city to shop around, but actually, he is giving Gabriel and Mary some privacy, as they have much to talk about and need to get reacquainted.

Gabriel asks John if he is going to contact his family back in the states, and he indicates that he has already contacted his mother. John then says, "I will be back in a couple of hours, so don't worry about me."

As John shuts the door, Gabriel and Mary sit on the couch and just stare at each other. As Gabriel stares at Mary, he cannot believe how beautiful she is, and he has an instant flashback to when he first saw Mary all dressed up and ready to go to the senior prom with Chad.

For the next couple of hours, they talk about each other's lives. Mary tells Gabriel that after the announcement that his airplane was lost, she also went into a depression and received counseling for around six months.

"I never came to the belief that you were actually gone. I just had an instinct about it. I then enrolled in the state college and received my nursing degree. After one year at the local hospital, I had a calling to help those less fortunate, so I signed up to come here. I don't know why I picked this exact hospital, and I never questioned my decision."

Gabriel tells Mary about every event that has happened in the past six years, including the airplane crash, his surrogate family on the island, how the gorilla saved his life, the accident in the cave, how he was rescued on the island, meeting John and the sinking of the merchant marine ship, the life raft, and then making it to the hospital.

Gabriel then says to Mary, "You know, finding each other here is not just a coincidence but is fate. We were destined to meet here by design, for what reason neither of us knows, but whatever it is, we are to face it as partners in life. God has a plan for us, and it will be real interesting where we go from here."

As they complete the discussions about their lives, they then kiss and embrace each other. Early in the evening, John returns to the apartment and enjoys a delicious dinner that Mary has prepared for them. After dinner, Mary prepares a bed on the couch for John, and then they retire for the evening.

CHAPTER 21

It is the next morning, Saturday to be exact, and Mary has the weekend off. Mary has prepared breakfast, and sitting at the table are Gabriel and John, discussing what their immediate plans are to be. John has indicated that he is to fly back to the states to see his mother and just relax for the next couple of weeks. John then asks Gabriel, "What are your plans?"

Gabriel looks at Mary and takes her hand in his, looks at John, and says, "I am not sure, as it has been over six years that I have not had to just be in survival mode. I believe that I should return home to see my parents rather than just call them on the phone. It will be quite an emotional time, and I must do it right away."

John says, "Why don't we fly out together?"

Gabriel then looks at Mary and says, "I can't go without you. I will never leave your side again.

Mary smiles at Gabriel and says, "I will call the hospital and make arrangements to have another nurse take over my duties."

Later that day, Mary informs Gabriel and John that their flight departs for Miami tomorrow morning and Gabriel must purchase some new clothes to wear for the trip. John is already wearing some new clothes that he had purchased yesterday and states that he will stay at the apartment while they go shopping. Gabriel and Mary know that John is just trying to be considerate of their privacy and insist that they all go together. John agrees, and they all depart for city center. As the day goes on, the three have a good time shopping and have a lot of laughs as Gabriel tries on some wild and funky clothes.

At day's end, they dine at Lamin Lodge, and Mary is asked to order for everyone. It is a local meal (ceebu jen) that is one of her favorites. The meal consists of an herbed grouper steak prepared with vegetables and rice, and for dessert, they have lemon custard.

When they return to Mary's apartment, they all retire early, as tomorrow will be a busy day and they must be at the airport early in the morning so as not to miss their flight. Prior to their departure, Mary calls her parents and informs them when she will be arriving and tells them that she will be with a special friend. Mary's parents are very excited that Mary is coming home, as it has been over one year since they have all been together. Pamela enquires about this special friend, and Mary tells her that it is someone they have known for many years and not to be shocked when they see him. When they hang up the phone, Pamela and Tom are puzzled as to who this person might be, as they know all of Mary's school friends and cannot think of who he is.

As they board the airplane and take their assigned seats, they are all sitting together at the request of Mary when she made the reservations. The flight is non-stop, and for Gabriel and Mary, this doesn't seem to bother them at all. With the exception of taking a few short naps, they hold hands, smile, and laugh a lot and have a chance to just sit and talk about everything that has happened in their lives, including the first day in kindergarten when they met.

Just prior to landing, Mary calls her folks and tells them that they are scheduled to arrive within thirty minutes and can meet them in the passenger arrival area at the lower level next to the luggage claim section. As they depart the plane and walk down the airport terminal, there are masses of people going in every direction, and Gabriel is somewhat taken aback at the sight, as he is unaccustomed to being in a crowded area and around this many people.

As they make their way downstairs to await Mary's parents, John says he is taking a connecting flight and must now say good-bye. He gives Mary a big hug and thanks her for everything and then turns to Gabriel. As he looks at Gabriel, he immediately gets teary eyed and says, "What can I say to the person that has saved my life? Gabriel, you risked your life for me when we were stranded in the ocean. You swam over and pulled me on the raft when I was about to give up. I also know one other time that you saved my life."

Gabriel, with a puzzled look on his face, says, "John, how can that be, as we only knew each other for a short time prior to that event?"

John says, "Gabe, I now know that it was you who put your hand on my shoulder in the schoolyard when we were in grade school."

Without any change in expression, Gabriel looks directly into John's eyes and has an instant recall of the event some nineteen years earlier. Mary looks at John and says, "My God, that was you in the schoolyard?"

John says, "Yes. Unfortunately, I was the school bully with many personal issues going on in my life."

Gabriel takes his hand, again places it on John's shoulder, and says "The good Lord has big plans for your future, and you must follow your heart."

John takes his hand and places it on Gabriel's and says, "I really do believe that, and I'm looking forward to new challenges. Maybe someday I will be able to repay you for your courage and healing touch."

The two men embrace in friendship, as this is now a bond that cannot be broken. They exchange addresses and phone numbers, and Gabriel tells John that he will soon be in contact. John again says thanks for everything and departs to locate his connecting flight. Mary and Gabriel just stand there, looking at each other, with Mary somewhat in disbelief at what John has just shared with them.

When Mary recognizes her parents' car, she tells Gabriel to stand just inside the terminal doors so they cannot see him. The car drives up in front, and both Tom and Pamela get out of the car and give Mary a big hug and kiss. They look around the area but cannot see who Mary's mysterious friend might be.

Mary tells them to turn around, with their backs to the terminal doors, and says, "I am warning you ahead of time that this person is going to be quite a shock to you."

Tom and Pamela look at each other with puzzled looks on their faces, not knowing why they are playing this little game that Mary is putting them through. Mary signals for Gabriel to come out and then tells her parents to turn around. As Gabriel approaches, Tom and Pamela turn and see who Mary's mysterious friend is. With shocked looks on their faces, they cannot believe what they are seeing.

"Oh my God! How can this be? Gabriel, is it really you?" says Pamela.

Gabriel walks right up to them, and all three embrace and have tears of happiness. With wide smiles, all three stand and just look at each other as Tom and Pamela wipe their tears in disbelief.

After a short time of digesting what is happening, Tom says, "Let's get in the car and go home."

Pamela tells Gabriel that she has a thousand questions to ask him, and Gabriel explains in short detail how he survived.

Pamela says, "Let's all get together with your parents for dinner tomorrow night at our house, and we can discuss all that has happened."

They drive for another fifteen minutes, and when they arrive at Gabriel's house, no one is home.

Pamela says, "I know where your parents are. They are at church. Your mother never misses evening services on this particular day, as it is the same day of the week that you were believed to have died."

When they arrive at Bethany Church, the only car in the parking lot is Joseph and Sarah's. As they enter the church, the low lighting gives a peaceful feeling of privacy. They see the altar area, which is lit by many candles, and a large stained glass cross that provides an ambiance of spirituality and peace.

While standing at the rear of the church, Gabriel sees his dad sitting in the front pew, with his head slightly bowed and his left hand on his forehead, and his mother kneeling in prayer at the base of the large crucifix. As Gabriel slowly approaches, he looks down on his father, who does not see him. Gabriel sits down next to his father and just stares at him. Joseph, sensing that someone is there, looks to his left and sees Gabriel right in front of him. At first, he doesn't seem to recognize Gabriel and has a blank look on his face. Then, all at once, he realizes it is his son, hugs him, and begins to cry.

Gabriel puts his finger to his own lips, signaling to his father that he must be quiet so Gabriel can go to his mother. Gabriel stands and walks up behind his mother, who is still kneeling in prayer. He kneels down beside his mother and does not say a word.

Sarah, who is in deep prayer, does not even know that Gabriel is beside her and continues to pray. After about thirty seconds, Sarah senses that she is not alone, but she does not look to see who this person might be. After a few more seconds, she glances to her left and sees a young man praying, but she cannot see his face.

Just then, Gabriel turns his head and looks directly into his mother's eyes. As their eyes meet, it is like Sarah is in a trance and cannot process what she is seeing. After a few seconds, her body goes completely limp, with her head dropping and her shoulders slumping forward. She begins to fall, and Gabriel catches her into his arms.

With her head now on Gabriel's chest, she slowly turns her head upward. Her eyes slowly open, and tears flow onto Gabriel's arms and hands, which embrace her. It is a sight that cannot even be expressed, the love of a mother for her son, a son that was thought to have been taken from her and now, by the grace of God, has been returned.

Sarah cries and says in a weak and sorrowful voice, "I have been praying to God since you were taken from me, and He has now answered my prayers. Gabriel, I have always known that you would come back home, and I have tried so very hard to hang on. Thank you Christ, for this wonderful gift, as you have brought my loving son back home to me." Joseph now walks up to Gabriel and Sarah, gets down on his knees, embraces them both, and sobs almost out of control. It is truly the most touching scene one could ever imagine

As the three embrace, a cross appears on

Gabriel's forehead, and his tears turn to blood. Mary and her parents stand in the aisle a few rows back from the altar and see the cross appear on Gabriel. When this happens, Mary's parents are in disbelief, but they know Gabriel has been blessed by God. After a short period of time, both families collectively embrace, smiling and crying. They depart the church, each going to their own home, with Joseph and Sarah graciously accepting the dinner invitation from Tom and Pamela.

CHAPTER 22

It is the next morning, and Gabriel and Joseph are sitting at the kitchen table enjoying a cup of hot coffee while Sarah is standing over the range/oven cooking breakfast. Sarah has a smile and look of happiness on her face that has not been present since the days when they were a happy loving family prior to the accident. The smell of bacon frying in the pan, biscuits baking in the oven at 350 degrees, and steam coming out of the old coffee pot, giving off an inviting coffee bean aroma, were like old times.

This day has the appearance of Christmas morning, and the greatest gift of all was delivered to Joseph and Sarah, the gift of their son Gabriel. However, this could not be a gift from Santa but only a gift that God Himself could deliver. Within a few minutes, they are seated at the kitchen table, their plates full of the hot, delicious, steaming food that Sarah has prepared.

As they are about to indulge in their meal, they all hold hands, creating a circle of energy, bow their heads, and Joseph leads them in prayer. "Dear Christ, our Heavenly Father, words cannot express how much love we have for You and as a family. When Gabriel was born, You blessed us with the greatest gift of all, a beautiful baby boy. We know You have a special plan for Gabriel and that You have chosen him to be a healer and messenger of Your truth and faith. Christ, please continue to protect Gabriel, as we know that he will again soon be leaving us to continue to do Your work. We love and believe in You with all of our heart and soul. In Jesus' name, we pray. Amen."

For the remainder of the day, Joseph, Sarah, and Gabriel stay at home and leisurely enjoy their time together. As the day progresses, it is time to depart to Tom and Pamela's for dinner. As they arrive, Tom and Pamela greet them at the door and share hugs and smiles, and Joseph hands Pamela a nice bottle of Chambertin-Clos de Bèze burgundy, which will go well with the London broil that she has prepared.

Gabriel then sees Mary smiling and walking out of the kitchen towards him, and a look of love and happiness immediately encompasses his face. The two then approach each other, embrace, and share a short, passionate kiss in a manner that one would expect for a couple in love.

For the next thirty minutes, they all enjoy hors d'oeuvres, wine, and each other's company. As the dinner's main course is completed, Sarah serves Gabriel's favorite dessert, which is, of course, lemon pie, and they also enjoy freshly ground, roasted Lavazza coffee, which is expensive and popular in Italy and served at exactly 155 degrees. As they enjoy the dessert and hot coffee, Tom asks Gabriel if he would share his experiences since the accident.

At this moment, the room becomes quiet, and as Gabriel looks around the table, he sees that all eyes are on him. Gabriel then folds his hands and places them in his lap, glances downward, clears his throat, and his eyes become glassy and tear up.

As Gabriel begins to talk, he first speaks of how difficult it was to see all of the people that had perished on the plane and how it seemed surreal. "At first, after the crash, when on the plane and seeing all of the lifeless people lying everywhere, I thought to myself, 'How could God have let this happen and spare only my life? What did these people do or not do in life that ended their lives so tragically?' There were even small children on the plane, and I became angry with God and cursed at Him. I thought that a just God would not have let this happen. I also felt guilty that I survived. But why me? I am no different than any other person on the plane. As I slept on the plane amongst all of the dead bodies, I remember praying and crying myself to sleep. Then, in my sleep, I had a dream, and God spoke to me. He explained to me that He had not caused the accident, but that it was Free Will, that fate had taken place, and it was their time to depart this earth. But for me, He had a plan. However, He did not explain what this plan was. I then remember opening my eyes, and from there, survival and trying to locate any other people on the island was my main objective."

Gabriel then explains how, on meeting the tribal people, they adopted him and that he had saved the tribal leader's child; how he encountered the injured large silverback gorilla in the cave and how the gorilla later saved his life from the tiger; how he became injured in the cave and almost did not survive; then how he was rescued by the Merchant Marine crew and the sinking of the ship.

He also talks about how John and he were stranded on a raft and were finally found by the natives of Guinea-Bissau. Then, as fate would have it, Mary was the attending nurse of the life flight that responded to the emergency request.

Mary then states that she was not scheduled to assist in the emergency recovery. "I just remember that I overheard the call come in, and for some unknown reason, at that time, I volunteered. I usually never assist in recoveries and stay at the hospital, as that is what my duties are. When I first saw Gabriel, I did not recognize him, as he had long hair, a long beard, and was thin. Then, when I realized it was Gabriel, I almost passed out and knew that all of my past prayers had finally been answered."

As everyone is now quietly sitting at the table, staring at Gabriel, thinking to themselves and realizing what Gabriel had encountered within the past six years, all know that God certainly protected him and that He has a future plan for him, that God, in His infinite wisdom, has had Gabriel experience all that he has, and they now wonder what new life experiences will be in store not only for him, but also Mary, who will, of course, be by his side from now on.

CHAPTER 23

It is now two days later, and all of the news commentators and government officials have discovered that Gabriel was the only survivor on Flight #23 that crashed over six years ago. The authorities contacted Gabriel and an interview is to be held downtown at the Federal Building.

The entire large room is filled with local and national newscasters, officials from the F.A.A., and some relatives and friends of those that perished on the flight. As Gabriel enters the room, it is noisy, with everyone talking, and he can see all of the television cameras and tables in front of the room, with one empty seat that was meant for him. As they walk toward the tables, Mary and his parents are escorted to the seats designated for them. Gabriel is then seated by one of the staff, and there, directly in front of and facing him, are four men in suits and one woman, who are all seated at a long table, staring at him.

As Gabriel takes his seat, the entire room becomes quiet. One of the men then introduces himself, welcomes and thanks Gabriel for attending, and indicates that they are on a fact-finding mission regarding Flight #23. Gabriel should have been somewhat nervous with all of the attention and cameras on him. However, he is very reserved and has a sense of calmness about him considering what he endured over the past six years.

As the questions are asked over the next hour, Gabriel answers them in great detail. Then the woman interviewer says, "There is a question that I and everyone here in attendance would like answered, and that is: why were you the only survivor in this terrible plane crash?"

With folded hands, Gabriel looks down, pauses, and does not say a word. Gabriel knows why he was spared. However, how could he answer, "Because God protected me and not the others on the flight. It would sound extremely arrogant on his part, and it appeared that this might have been a "setup question," one that might cause much controversy and skepticism about him.

Gabriel then reverses the question on the woman and says, "Why do you think I was spared? Why would only one person survive such a horrible accident? If it were you that was sitting here and not I, how would you answer this question? For a long time, I asked myself the same question and figured that it was just my lucky time to hit the lottery, and that was the lottery of life. However, as I was a survivor on that small island, I came to realize the real answer. I personally now know the answer. However, that is private between God and myself."

The woman then says, "Please, answer just one more question for us. I have been doing some research on your life from where you went to school, your personal interests, and all of the activities you participated in through high school. Two particular events happened in your life that was quite interesting and extraordinary. The first is when you saved the life of the principal of your high school, who, by the way, is doing quite well even to this day, and the second is when you saved Mary Hart's life, who, I understand, is now your fiancé and here today. According to the hospital and doctors that I interviewed, this was truly a miracle and one that is still unexplained to this day. Can you explain these occurrences for us here today?"

Gabriel again immediately realizes that the woman interviewer is trying to set him up, either to look like some kind of kook or a truly a blessed person with some kind of spiritual powers. Gabriel then pauses in deep thought and says, "I don't understand what these past events in my life have anything to do with the plane crash. I hope that I have answered everyone's questions today."

Gabriel then stands up from his chair, and a voice from the back of the room yells out, "My daughter and small grandchild were on that flight. Do you remember seeing them?" Then another loud voice is heard asking if he remembers a man in a dark suit and blue tie.

Out of respect for the friends and relatives of the deceased, Gabriel holds up his hand and says, "I will be available to answer questions for those that lost loved ones up here at the table."

At that moment, many people rush towards him, and not only the friends and relatives of the victims of the plane crash, but also the news media immediately surround him. The majority of the people want to shake his hand, pat him on the back, and congratulate him for surviving such an ordeal.

Gabriel then says, "I now only want to speak to those that lost loved ones, and I will not answer any more questions from the media."

Then, as the surrounding crowd thins out, there are a number of people still remaining with all eyes on him. There, directly in front of him, is a small, gray-haired, elderly woman with a cane, looking up at Gabriel with glassy eyes. He places his hand on her shoulder, looks down on her, and says, "Is there a question that I can answer for you?"

The woman says, "Were there any passengers that could have possibly survived the plane crash with you?"

Gabriel then has an immediate flashback of all of the deceased bodies on the plane and knows that his answer to her must be honest yet comforting. He then explains that while all perished on the flight, no one suffered. As he is looking directly at the woman, her eyes immediately fill with tears. She cries and slowly drops to her knees. Gabriel then crouches down and embraces the woman in his arms, and his eyes then fill with tears. He whispers into her ear, "God is with your son, Jay, and he is happy and with our Creator and wants you to know this."

The woman then looks directly into Gabriel's eyes and says, "How did you know I had a son named Jay on the plane?"

Gabriel smiles at the woman and says, "I sat next to Jay on the plane, and he spoke about you and the loving family he had."

The woman places her hand on Gabriel's face, gently kisses him on the cheek, and says, "Thank you for your kind words, as I finally have closure and know that my son is safe and at peace."

He helps her to her feet, and she takes her handkerchief and wipes the tears off of Gabriel's cheeks and notices that her handkerchief has been stained slightly red. She looks at him again and slowly walks out of the room.

For the next thirty minutes, Gabriel explains to

the remaining people about the crash and tries to console everyone who is still in attendance. As the last person leaves, Mary walks up to Gabriel with tears also in her eyes, as she has been listening to the conversations. She holds his hand, and they walk out together.

CHAPTER 24

It is the next day, and Mary and Gabriel are at their favorite fast food restaurant (Yaw's), the one they and their friends frequented often when in high school. As they are sitting at the table waiting for their food to be served, Gabriel looks directly into Mary's eyes, takes her hand in his, and says, "There is something that I want to ask you."

Mary looks at Gabriel and says, "You are scaring me, as you look so serious."

Gabriel then gets down on one knee in front of Mary, takes out a small black box from his pocket, opens it, and there is a beautiful diamond ring. Mary immediately gets teary-eyed and loudly says, "YES."

Gabriel laughs and says, "I haven't even asked you the question yet. Maybe I'm going to ask you to pay for lunch or mend the hole in my underwear."

Mary, who is now so excited that she can hardly sit still, says, "I will be happy to buy lunch and mend your old, holey underwear." Mary, still grinning from ear to ear says, "Okay, Gabriel, what do you want to ask me?"

Gabriel again gets his serious face on and says, "Mary, I have loved you since the day we met and will always love and cherish you. Will you honor me by becoming my bride and wife?"

Mary, now trying to compose herself by keeping a semi-straight face, pauses and then says, "Can I think about it?"

Gabriel, still looking at Mary, has a blank look on his face. Then Mary begins to laugh, Gabriel begins to laugh, and they both hug and kiss in happiness. Then, in the next instant, all of the people sitting at the neighboring tables and booths watching and hearing the entire event unfold all stand and applaud.

After they finish lunch, they first go to Mary's house, and she tells her parents the good news and shows off her new ring. However, they already knew this was going to happen, as Gabriel had asked Tom for permission to have Mary's hand in marriage. They then go to Gabriel's house, and Mary again shows off her new ring to Joseph and Sarah.

Joseph says, "Let me call Tom and Pam and have us all meet at Jake's Crawfish for dinner tonight to celebrate, and dinner and drinks are on us."

At dinner that night, both Joseph and Tom give toasts as they all enjoy a delicious meal of lobster, salmon, and halibut steaks. As they are having dessert, Gabriel and Mary announce that they have decided on a small wedding, so small, in fact, that only the six of them will be present. The wedding is planned for one week from tomorrow, which will be a Sunday at Bethany church, and is scheduled for 5:00 p.m.

The next few days just seem to fly by as Mary, Pam, and Sarah enjoy shopping and finding Mary a dress and also buying new dresses for themselves. During that week, Gabriel has been in contact with Christian sponsors who might be interested in financing a Christian Mission to Rwanda. While talking on the telephone to one group of sponsors, they realize that Gabriel is the lone survivor of the plane crash and set up an appointment to meet with him on Wednesday at the Red Lion hotel by the Lloyd Center mall.

Wednesday quickly arrives, and Gabriel goes to the front desk of the hotel and is instructed to go down the hall to the Willamette room, which is a convention area for seminars and company meetings. As Gabriel opens the door and enters the room, he is quite surprised by the number of people that are in attendance, as he thought that only a couple of people would be there to meet with him.

As he walks in the room, several men in suits immediately greet him. They smile and shake Gabriel's hand and thank him for coming. Gabriel does not know what to think, as he was the one trying to recruit their services, not the other way around. As they walk with Gabriel towards the people in attendance, he is then individually introduced to everyone with a smile and a handshake. Overall, there are thirty people there to meet with him, twenty men and ten women. As they all take their seats at the large, circular table, Gabriel is seated next to the director, Mr. Steven.

Mr. Steven thanks everyone for attending and also thanks Gabriel. He then explains the purpose of the meeting that this is to be a question-and-answer session. He then goes on to tell Gabriel that they are a Christian group, a co-op of a number of different Christian organizations with the same purpose and goal: to go to Rwanda as a Christian missionary, to meet with the people of that region, and to teach the Christian message, that Jesus Christ is the Savior, and to bring hope and spirituality to the people.

As the meeting goes on for about one hour, there are also numerous questions for the director from those in attendance regarding what Gabriel's additional roles and duties are to be as a Christian missionary. Mr. Steven indicates a list of duties, which includes assisting in their living conditions, irrigation, and food preservation, providing medical assistance, and, of course, acting as a spiritual leader. Mr. Steven then looks at Gabriel and asks him if he thinks he is qualified to perform all of these duties.

Gabriel then goes on to tell about his life when stranded on the island and how he assisted and lived with a tribe and performed all of the duties that would be expected of him. Mr. Steven then asks, "What about the medical aspect? The native people will require vaccinations and other medical treatment of their conditions, some of which could be quite serious."

Gabriel says, "My fiancé, Mary, who is to become my wife this weekend, is a registered RN and has been working at the Royal North Shore Hospital in Lamin, Guinea. I also have a friend that I can contact who has been a corpsman with the Merchant Marines and who could assist in all of the needed duties. He is very qualified and a person I would trust with my life."

Mr. Steven looks around the table and asks if there are any more questions for Gabriel. A woman then raises her hand and says, "I have just one last question I would like to ask. When I saw your interview the other day on the television with the FAA and other local officials, you were asked about a couple of extraordinary events that took place earlier in your life, and you declined to answer. Would you please explain what transpired, as I am sure all of us here in attendance would like to know the circumstances of the events?"

The immediate thought that runs through Gabriel's mind is that this is another setup question that if answered incorrectly in their minds, might disqualify him from receiving this very important assignment.

Gabriel looks down, momentarily pauses, and then looks up at the woman and says, "What I am about to tell you is extremely private in my life. It is only because I want to go to Rwanda to teach the word of God and Jesus and assist in the lives of the underprivileged and needy that I will answer your question."

As Gabriel is about to speak, all eyes are on him, and the room is so quiet that you could have heard a pin drop. Gabriel then tells of the situation with Mr. Kleiner, the school principal, and his role in bringing him back to life. He then tells of the event with Mary, how he visited the morgue, how she was pronounced dead, and how all of the bones in her body were broken.

As Gabriel takes a quick glance around the table, he sees expressions of disbelief, with raised eyebrows, pressed lips, and frowning faces, and some people have no expression at all.

The woman looks at Gabriel and says, "That is a pretty extraordinary story that you tell. It seems that in your mind, you have the power of Jesus, to heal and bring the dead back to life. You have to admit, Mr. Adams, it is really difficult to believe such stories that you have just shared with us."

At this time, Mr. Steven has his head down, looking at his hands folded and resting on the table, and he is somewhat at a loss for words, and nothing is said for the next ten seconds.

The woman then says, "All right, Mr. Adams, if you have such a power, then prove it to all of us right now. Perform a miracle."

Gabriel now realizes that this is what he feared: the question is a setup to make him look unstable and like he has delusions of grandeur. Gabriel now slightly scoots his seat back, stands up, and looks directly into the eyes of the woman. He could have become angry and walked out of the room. However, Gabriel does not need to prove himself to her or any other person. His polite comment to her is "Ma'am, I am not a dog and pony show, and I do not need to perform a sideshow for you. Your request of me just tells and shows me what is in your heart. No, what is not in your heart."

The lady replies, "But your healing powers sound preposterous, and if I can't see such miracles firsthand, then, to me, they are just made up stories that I don't believe."

A slight smile now appears on Gabriel's face,

and he says, "Did you see the miracles that Jesus performed, and did you see Him die on the cross? If your statement is true and you did not witness these events, then how can you believe the Bible?"

The woman momentarily pauses and then says, "Because I have faith."

Gabriel then says, "Yes, that is exactly the right answer, you have faith. I also have faith that Jesus is the Son of God, and I believe in the Bible and the miracles that happened, but I did not see them happen. However, I don't take the Bible as literally as it is written. It doesn't matter to me if events happened exactly as written. I only know that in my heart, Jesus does exist, and He is the way to everlasting life. The last six years of my life were not events that just happened randomly and without purpose. God has tested and protected me, and He has a plan for the remainder of my life. I believe that He has a plan for all of our lives. However, our journeys take us all on different paths that we must experience for ourselves. I do not know what His future plans are for me. However, I do know that in His infinite wisdom, I will never question where He leads me. The will of God will never take you where the grace of God will not protect you. If it is that all of you here in attendance have confidence in me and would like me to be your representative, then that is great, and I would be honored. However, it is not with you that I would be employed, but rather Christ. If you feel that I am not the right person and do not meet your standards, then I completely understand, and I will just have to continue my search elsewhere."

He then turns to his right and puts out his hand to Mr. Steven, smiles, shakes his hand, and thanks him for his hospitality and consideration. As Gabriel leaves and walks towards the exit doors, the room is completely quiet, as no one around the table says a word.

CHAPTER 25

The big day has finally arrived, Sunday afternoon, and Gabriel, Joseph, Sarah, and Pamela are at the church annex. However, Gabriel has not yet seen Mary, as tradition has it that it is bad luck for the groom to see the bride on the day prior to the wedding ceremony. The church annex is a private, small chapel extension of the church, which has a few bench seats and a built-in stained glass cross on the wall that is illuminated by the outside sunlight.

As Joseph, Sarah, and Pamela are seated, and Gabriel and Pastor Maragelis are standing at the altar, the door opens, and Mary enters, escorted by her father, Tom. Mary is dressed in a beautiful white satin chiffon wedding dress. She looks absolutely gorgeous, and with her natural beauty, she could be on the cover of any bride's magazine. As they take the short walk to the altar, Gabriel cannot take his eyes off of Mary and is in awe of her beauty.

As they arrive the altar, Pastor Maragelis asks, "Who gives this woman to be presented to this man?"

Tom then states, "Her mother and I do." Mary gives her father a kiss on the cheek and then turns toward Gabriel and presents her hand to him. Gabriel now takes her hand in his and is smiling from ear to ear.

Pastor Maragelis now proceeds to talk about their future lives together and what is expected of each in their marriage. He now says, "I believe that each of you have written your own vows, so who would like to go first?"

Mary then states that she would like to speak first. As Gabriel and Mary turn towards each other, they continue to hold hands. Mary now has a serious look on her face, and Gabriel is smiling. As they look into each other's eyes, Mary says in a slightly trembling voice, "My darling Gabriel, I love you, and I want to share my entire life with you. I will seek to share my deepest thoughts and self with you. I promise to love you for eternity and provide you with all of the care and support through all of life's challenges that we shall endure together. Gabriel, you are my protector and knight in shining armor. I now realize that ever since the day we met, I have always loved you, and it is through God's will that we wed. That through God's pure Spirit and wisdom, we together shall be bountiful in life and always have Christ in our hearts and souls to guide us as long as we shall live." Mary now places the ring on Gabriel's finger.

Gabriel, now with teary eyes, looks deeply into Mary's eyes and says, "Mary, you are the love of my life, and I have loved you since the first day I saw your blond hair and big blue eyes sitting next to me in kindergarten. With every heartbeat and every breath of my being, I promise to love and cherish you, to comfort and honor you and gladly give my life to protect you. In Christ's infinite wisdom, He has joined us to be a loving couple to encounter all of life's challenges together. My love for you will continue to grow and be as fresh as each morning day in spring." Gabriel, still with tears in his eyes, now places the ring on the finger of Mary, who has tears running down her cheeks.

The pastor now says, "It is my honor to present to the world Mr. and Mrs. Adams. Gabriel, you may now kiss your beautiful bride."

As Gabriel and Mary's lips touch, it is almost surreal what transpires. They have the same vision, and it is as if their future life together flashes before them, but in slow motion if that makes any sense. After the kiss and embrace, they both now turn and are greeted by their parents with additional hugs and kisses and, of course, teary eyes from all.

After the wedding ceremony, they all go to the Benson Hotel for a wonderful dinner. After dinner, a hotel staff member escorts Gabriel and Mary up to their room. As they enter the room, the mood is set with a welcome bottle of sparkling wine, chocolate-dipped strawberries, and rose petals scattered across the bed.

After the staff member opens the bottle of sparkling wine and pours some into two glasses, he excuses himself and begins to depart. Gabriel stops him, gives him a generous tip, and thanks him for his service. Gabriel then takes the two glasses of wine and hands one to Mary. They touch glasses in celebration, take a sip of the wine, and just stare at each other.

Mary now excuses herself and says that she would like to change out of her wedding dress into something more comfortable. As she is changing, Gabriel also changes into comfortable night-lounging clothes and robe. As Gabriel waits, he begins to feel lightheaded. However, it is not from the sparkling wine but from some anxiety and nervousness.

Just then, Mary walks back into the room. She is wearing a beautiful red negligee. However, it is partially hidden by a white silk nightgown that extends to the floor. Mary takes her glass, and they both proceed to finish their glass of bubbly. At this moment, there is a slight feeling of awkwardness from both, as, you see, Gabriel and Mary are virgins. Mary now walks right up to Gabriel, puts her arms around his neck, and just stares at him. As Gabriel is looking into Mary's blue eyes, it is like he is hypnotized and in a trance, and the feeling of nervousness immediately vanishes. They have a long, passionate kiss, and Gabriel then picks Mary up in his arms, carries her to the bed, and gently lays her down. He pushes the remote control button for the room lighting, and it becomes immediately semi-dark. He lies down beside her, and they embrace one another. This is a long overdue moment in each other's lives together and is a time not of just love for one another, but also of deep emotion and passion. Throughout the remainder of the night and into early morning, Gabriel and Mary consummate their marriage numerous times to be sure they get it right.

CHAPTER 26

It is now two days later, and Gabriel and Mary are packing the car to travel to the beach for their short honeymoon. Their plans are to travel to the central coastline, which is Lincoln City, and then venture north towards Seaside and Astoria and spend a couple of nights at each town.

As they are saying their good-byes to Joseph and Sarah, the phone rings, and Sarah answers the call. She then looks at Gabriel and says, "The call is for you, and I don't recognize the voice."

Gabriel answers and says, "Hi, this is Gabriel." As he listens intensely to the caller, his expression goes from a questionable look to an appearance of almost shock as his eyebrows raise, and then he begins to smile. As Mary, Joseph, and Sarah watch Gabriel's reaction to the caller, they are in suspense of what is being said. At the end of the conversation, Gabriel says, "Yes, sir, thank you for calling, and we will see you then."

As Gabriel hangs up the phone, Mary says, "You have a look of astonishment on your face. What was that all about?"

Gabriel looks at Mary and says, that was Mr. Steven from the Christian co-op that I interviewed with last week. He said that after I left the meeting, the vote was 30 to zero, and they want to sponsor us to be their missionaries to Rwanda. How about that? Even the skeptic lady voted for us."

Mary and Gabriel laugh, grab one another, and start jumping up and down in complete happiness that they have been selected. Gabriel takes a piece of paper from his wallet, picks up the phone, and says, "I must call John and tell him what is happening. I surely hope that he will be interested and available so we can make the tour together."

Gabriel calls John and explains everything to him and that the meeting is scheduled for a week from Thursday. John also sounds excited and says, "I will fly in next Wednesday and will let you know my flight number." As Gabriel hangs up the phone, he still has a look of shock on his face, as he cannot believe what has just happened.

For the next six days, Gabriel and Mary travel and sightsee the beautiful western coastline and, of course, behave as honeymooners should by being completely immersed in each other.

The following Wednesday, Gabriel and Mary arrive at the airport and meet John at the luggage claim area. All three hug with big smiles, gather John's luggage, load it into the car, and arrive at Joseph and Sarah's house just in time for dinner.

As they enter the house, John is introduced to Joseph and Sarah and Tom and Pamela, who are also there. An inviting aroma of a variety of food items enhances the air, which would make any palate yearn to taste the tantalizing food. When dinner is served, they see that Sarah has prepared a meal fit for a king, with prime rib, twice baked potatoes, green bean casserole, oven-roasted asparagus, Caesar salad, and dinner rolls and for dessert a cheesecake covered with strawberries that seems to melt in their mouths.

As the evening progresses, they sit around the table and talk, laugh, and continue to drink Sarah's ground roasted Lavazza coffee. As the evening comes to an end at around 10:00 p.m., Tom and Pamela give thanks and hugs to Sarah and Joseph, shake John's hand and wish him good luck, and then hug Mary and Gabriel. Within a couple of minutes, Sarah and Joseph excuse themselves and retire for the evening.

For the next hour, Gabriel and Mary sit on the couch and John in the chair, and they discuss what is to be in store for them and are excited about the meeting tomorrow with Mr. Steven. In bed that night, Gabriel lies wide awake, staring up at the dark ceiling as a million thoughts run through his head.

CHAPTER 27

It is Thursday morning, around 11:00 a.m. and Gabriel, Mary, and John meet with Mr. Steven at his downtown office on Broadway Street. As Gabriel introduces Mary and John to Mr. Steven, they all shake hands and exchange pleasantries. For the next three hours, they go over the itinerary and have a working lunch, as there are many questions to be answered and certain schedule guidelines that must be understood.

As they finally finish the last explanation of the events that are to take place, Mr. Steven says, "The entire Christian co-op is very happy with their selection for you to represent our Christian organization." He then advises them, "Be careful, as you will be out of country and the United States has no jurisdiction. However, we do have representation for civilization employees. Also, occasionally, there are rebels that run slave trades through that area. However, typically, they never bother the missionaries unless provoked." Mr. Steven gives Gabriel his direct phone number by which he can be reached at any time, they all shake hands, and he wishes them good will and much success.

As they depart the building, they are all

excited. However, John and Mary feel a little overwhelmed, as there is much to do, with a big responsibility on all of them. Gabriel senses that they have this feeling. However, he does not say a word about it and knows that they will do great once they are truly involved with the whole process.

They must now be prudent with their time, as they are departing for Rwanda in just two days. The next two days seem to fly by, and soon, they are airborne, heading for their final destination. As they finally arrive at the Kigali airport in Rwanda, it is around 2:00 a.m. They are tired from the flight and experiencing jet lag. They walk through the airport to the baggage claim area, pick up their luggage, head for shuttle service, and board the bus to the Chez Lando hotel, which is just five minutes from the airport. As they arrive at the hotel, they are pleased to see that the café is open. They order and enjoy their meals, retire to their rooms, and are asleep within just minutes of when their heads hit the pillows.

The next morning, they meet again at the café, have breakfast, and discuss their plans for the day. Gabriel now calls Chinedu, who is the African liaison, and they meet him at an airport hangar where their supplies are stored. These are the supplies that must be flown in and dropped by parachute at the village where they have been assigned. After they inspect and verify that all of the supplies are accounted for, they are informed that their flight will be departing tomorrow morning at 8:00 a.m. Since they have the rest of the day to themselves, they decide to visit downtown Kigali, which is the capital city of Rwanda. Kigali is also the city that the horrible genocide took place that killed 800,000 people in 1994.

As the day comes to an end, they decide to dine at the Heaven Café, which was recommended by some of the local residents. At the café, they decide to try the traditional African cuisine with a variety of food dishes they can share. Their food order includes Kota (curry stuffed into a hollowed-out loaf of bread), boerewors (sausage that is barbecued), gatsby (long roll with fillings of polony, chicken and steak, and hot chips), gesmoorde vis (salted cod with potatoes and tomatoes), isidudu (pumpkin pap), trotters and beans (boiled pig's or sheep's feet, onions, and beans) and umvubo (sour milk mixed with dry pap.) As the food arrives at their table, their eyes widen with smiles on their faces as they welcome the inviting array of food dishes and aromas that have been presented before them. For the next thirty minutes, they indulge in the food and are pleasantly surprised by the wonderful differing tastes of each food item. As they complete their meals, there is not one item left on any of their plates, and they know they made a wise decision on their food choices.

They then walk back to the hotel, and Gabriel asks the staff person on duty that they be awakened at 5:30 a.m., as they must be at the airport hangar by 7:00 a.m. After such a big dinner and short walk back to the hotel, they are tired, decide to go right to bed, and are excited for their new adventure to begin.

CHAPTER 28

It is the next morning, and they have just departed the hotel shuttle bus right in front of the supply hangar. Within one minute, the hangar door opens, and out walks Chinedu, greeting them with a good morning and handshake. As they talk for the next five minutes, Gabriel gets a good sense about Chinedu, as his personality appears to be that of a humble and genuine person and someone that can be trusted. In general conversation, Gabriel asks him personal questions about himself and family.

Chinedu explains that he is a Christian, that his name means "God Is My Leader," that he has been married to his wife, Chima (God Knows), for fifteen years, and that he has two children, a son named Chinaza (God Answers), who is eight years old, and Chinwendu (God Owns Life), his daughter, who is six years old. He then pulls out his wallet and with great pride shows Gabriel a family picture. As the picture illustrates, they are all smiling and appear to be a happy, normal family. However, as Gabriel looks deeply into Chinedu's eyes, he sees a slight tear and a shallow look on his face that only a trained eye would recognize.

Gabriel says to Chinedu "Is something wrong?"

Chinedu responds, "My daughter, Chinwendu,

was diagnosed with advanced leukemia two months ago, and it is breaking our hearts to watch her struggle, and she is continually getting weaker." Chinedu covers his face with his hands, trying to hide his tears, and as Gabriel watches him, the tears run down Chinedu's cheeks, escaping where his hands could not cover.

Gabriel takes a few steps toward him, embraces him, and says, "I am so sorry, as this must be very difficult for you and your wife."

Chinedu drops his hands from his face, wipes the tears from his eyes and cheeks with the back of his hand, and states, "It is very hard to watch your loving child suffer right before your eyes, and there is nothing we can do. She is in the hospital, and according to the doctor, if her chemotherapy treatments don't soon start to work, it could become fatal. I pray to God and ask that He please take me and let Chinwendu live, as she is so precious and loving."

Gabriel says, "Will you please take me to her, as I would like to meet her."

Chinedu looks at Gabriel and says, "That is very thoughtful of you, but your flight is soon to depart."

Gabriel states, "The flight can wait, and with your permission, I would like to meet your daughter."

Chinedu looks at Gabriel with a gentle smile and says, "My van is right around the corner of the hangar, and the hospital is just ten minutes away."

Mary and John also get in the van, and all four drive to the hospital and take the elevator to the third floor, which is the oncology ward. As they enter the room, Chinedu walks up to Chinwendu's bed, looks down on her frail body and baldhead as she is sleeping, and immediately gets teary-eyed. Slowly Gabriel, Mary, and John also walk to her bedside and say nothing.

As they are all looking down on her, Dr. Dubal enters the room. He walks up to Chinedu, shakes his hand, and his face is expressionless. Chinedu then introduces Dr. Dubal to Gabriel, Mary, and John, and they all greet one another. Dr. Dubal then states to Chinedu, "Unfortunately, the chemotherapy is not working, and there is nothing else that can be done."

Mary, who is an RN and familiar with the disease, asks Dr. Dubal the particulars of the cancer. He explains, "Chinwendu has a rare case of acute leukemia, one which is fast growing, with a large number of abnormal white blood cells that are produced in the bone marrow. These abnormal white cells have crowded the bone marrow and flooded the bloodstream, and I have never seen such a fast-growing cancer."

Mary then asks, "What about a bone marrow transplant?" Dr. Dubal explains, "Her rare form of cancer is so aggressive that a bone marrow transplant would be unsuccessful." He then says to Chinedu, "You should call your wife, as I believe that she has only a short time left. He excuses himself and says that he will be back soon to look in on her and leaves the room.

At this time, Gabriel, Mary, and John go out into the hallway, giving Chinedu some privacy. He then takes out his cell phone and calls his wife, Chima, and tells her that she must come up to the hospital. Within ten minutes, Chima hurriedly enters the room and grabs Chinedu's hand, and as they are looking down on Chinwendu, they both begin to cry. After about five minutes, Chinedu leaves the room, walks up to Gabriel, and apologizes that they have to experience what is happening.

Gabriel says, "Please, do not apologize to us for your unfortunate situation, as this time in your life is as difficult as it gets."

Within seconds, Chima opens the door and looks at Chinedu with a panicked look on her face. Chinedu looks at Gabriel and then quickly enters the room. Within another short time period, Dr. Dubal and a nurse quickly enter the room and do not depart for another ten minutes. The doctor then walks past

Gabriel, looks him straight in the eye, and shakes his head, indicating that she has just passed away.

The immediate thought that runs through Gabriel's mind is "I cannot just stand here and do nothing." He grabs Mary's hand, with John following, and they enter the room. As they approach the bed, both Chinedu and Chima are holding Chinwendu's hands. Their heads are bowed, and they are sobbing. Gabriel then walks over to the window and closes the blinds, making the room slightly dark. He walks over to her bedside and says to Chima, "Would you mind if I hold her hand?"

Chima releases her daughter's hand, and Gabriel then takes Chinwendu's hand in his, and all hold hands, creating a circle of energy to flow directly to Chinwendu's body. Gabriel then takes his other hand and places it on her forehead and begins to pray. At this time, everyone has their heads bowed and are listening to Gabriel's prayer.

"Dear Lord God, our Heavenly Father, I ask in Your name that You please release this child from the grasp of death so that she may live and have the opportunity to experience life to its fullest. Christ, she has been named Chinwendu, which means God Owns Life. I can feel in my heart that she loves and believes in You and, with Your blessing, will become one of Your Disciples and spread the Word of Your loving way, which leads to everlasting life. Christ, I ask that You please hear our prayer and we love and believe in you with all our heart and soul. Amen."

As Gabriel is leaning over Chinwendu, the sign of the cross appears on his forehead, and his tears of red blood fall gently onto her face, and he is crying not only for Chinwendu, also for the deep love that he has for Christ. Within a few seconds, the candle that is sitting on the stand beside her bed ignites and glows. With the shadowy effect on the walls from the glow of the candle, the appearance of wings in flight can be seen. As all are in witness of this blessed event, Mary and John have an instant recall of when Gabriel was about to die in the hospital.

As all are looking down on Chinwendu, her eyes open, and she smiles and says, "Mommy and Daddy, I just had a dream that I was in a dark tunnel, and then all of a sudden, there was a bright light, and a voice told me to follow it to the end, and that's all I can remember." She then sits up in bed and says, "I'm thirsty."

With big smiles on their faces and many tears, Chinedu and Chima now hug Chinwendu and realize that they have just experienced a holy miracle. Gabriel now goes over to the window and opens the blinds, creating a bright and cheerful room.

Chinedu and Chima approach Gabriel,

embrace him, and say, "How can we ever repay you for healing our daughter?"

Gabriel says, "It was not I that healed Chinwendu. Only God has the power to perform such a miracle. I am only the messenger."

Within a few minutes, Dr. Dubal enters the room and is in disbelief when he sees her sitting up in bed. For the next day, Chinwendu undergoes a series of examinations, with the final results showing no sign of cancer ever being present in her body.

CHAPTER 29

Their flight finally departs around 11:00 a.m. that morning. They are aboard a single-engine/propeller Cessna 172M, which makes for a cozy ride, as there is little wiggle room when also accounting for their luggage, which consists of only a few duffle bags of clothing. Their additional clothing, personal belongings, and all supplies will be parachuted to them soon after they arrive in the village area.

After around a two-hour flight deep into the jungle, the Cessna begins its final descent, and they now see ahead and below that the landing area is only a short grassy strip that has been cleared by the locals some years ago. The pilot, who calls himself Sky King and who wears a cowboy hat, informs them to hold on tight, as sometimes crosswinds blow through the area that can make for a bumpy landing.

As the plane descends to around two hundred feet, strong crosswinds grab the small Cessna and throw it around like it is a toy. Gabriel sees that the pilot is struggling to keep control of the airplane as they are all being thrown from side to side. The plane should now be at a 45-degree angle. However, it is coming in sideways due to the extreme turbulence.

As the pilot continues to struggle, he descends

to within one quarter-mile of the runway and has to turn the plane downward, slow to 80 to 85 knots, and have the engine powered to around 2,000 rpms so the plane will not stall out. When they are within fifty feet of the grassy landing strip, the pilot yells "Hold on!" As the plane tires hit the runway, Sky King yells out, "YAHOO", as if he is riding a bucking bronco. The landing is very bumpy and "scary" to say the least, and more exciting than any rollercoaster ride that they have ever experienced.

Once the plane is safely on the ground and at a standstill, Sky King looks at Gabriel, Mary, and John, and it is if he were looking at ghosts, all with white faces. The pilot says, "Thank you for flying Sky King Airlines, and we hope you have enjoyed your flight," and starts to laugh.

With shaky legs, they grab their bags, depart the airplane, and are met by three native tribesmen who do not speak English. One of the tribesmen hands Gabriel an envelope that has a letter of instruction inside. The instructions say, "These are your guides, who are to take you to the village that is approximately thirty minutes away."

As they then head into the jungle, lightning can be seen in the sky, and shortly thereafter, thunder can be heard off in the distance. After only ten minutes, warm rain begins to fall. However, they are partially protected by the heavy vegetation that surrounds them. By the time they reach the village, they are wet. However, they are not cold due to the high temperature, humidity, and rain that feels like a warm shower.

As they enter the village, all of the tribe's people come out to greet them, approximately two hundred in total. The community now surrounds them, and there are some smiles and chanting, which is part of the tribe's communication system.

Then one woman walks up to them, smiles, extends her hand, introduces herself as Mudiwa, and welcomes them in broken English. Mudiwa is the self-appointed caretaker of the village. Though her basic instincts as being the main figurehead are quite remarkable, she is at a great disadvantage with virtually no assistance from the outside-civilized world.

As they are all standing and slowly communicating, an airplane can be heard overhead. As they look up in the sky, they see parachutes with supplies are being dropped from the airplane. Gabriel now asks Mudiwa if she could instruct some of the tribesmen to assist them in bringing the supplies to the village. As the last of the supplies are brought in, Gabriel, Mary, and John now have a big job in unpacking and organizing all of the medical supplies, PVC irrigation piping, parts to assemble a water storage tank and filter, clothing, packaged food items, tools, and other numerous miscellaneous items. However, it is mid-afternoon, and they are hungry and tired, so they decide to wait until tomorrow to begin.

As night falls, they sit around the campfire, and can smell the aroma of stew that is cooking in clay pots over the fire. The stew consists of a mixture of various foods (vegetables and legumes) and is to be served over porridge made from cassava (root vegetable.) Also, they will be having steamed fish, which is prepared in leaf wrappers.

As they are served the food by some of the young females (which is tradition), they are quite surprised by the delicious taste of the food. However, John is accustomed to spicy food and asks if they have any seasonings that he might try. As instructed, one of the young girls leaves and shortly returns with a pepper-like substance.

Since the only light they have is that of the fire, John cannot see how much spice he sprinkles on the steamed fish. He then takes a sizeable bite of the fish and, for a few seconds, remains expressionless. Then, all of a sudden, his face turns bright red, he instantly begins to sweat, and his eyes widen to the size of saucers. He then opens his mouth, spits out the fish, yells out, and starts to run around the campfire like a wild man.

It is such a funny scene that the locals who are watching, including Gabriel and Mary, are laughing so hard that it brings tears to their eyes, with some of the natives actually rolling on the ground from laughter. You see, John has just ingested "Harissa," which is made of red birds-eye chili pepper, olive oil, garlic, cumin, and coriander. The tribesmen previously added more chili pepper, which makes it hotter than typical Harissa.

After a good laugh, they all decide to retire for the evening. However, John is up half the night ingesting food items with hopes of absorbing the heat and to diminish the furnace in his mouth.

CHAPTER 30

The next morning, Gabriel is up early and eager to begin unpacking all of the supplies, and shortly thereafter, Mary leaves the clay hut and joins him.

Mary says, "John will probably be up soon."

Gabriel, however, says, "He may not be up for a while. I heard him up last night walking around well into the early morning."

They both look at each other and laugh, as the scene with John last night was quite hilarious. As they walk to the campfire, which is the main cooking and gathering area for the entire tribe, they see Mudiwa and other women and young girls cooking, using the same clay pots that they have used for years. The clay pots work sufficiently, but Mary knows that some stainless steel cooking pots, fry pans, and kettles are part of the supplies that have been provided.

As they stand around the fire and discuss their plans for the day, John finally joins them, looking a little peaked and tired.

Mary looks at John and says, "You look a little tired. Did you not sleep well last night?"

As John looks at Mary, she smiles, and then John begins to slightly chuckle as he realizes how funny his sideshow last night must have appeared.

After they finish the morning breakfast, they go to the supplies that have been neatly stacked and begin to unpack the large canvas bags. For the next four hours, all three work diligently to unpack and organize the supplies, taking a lunch break and then continuing to work until dinnertime. After dinner, they retire early, as it has been a busy day, and tomorrow will be the same.

In fact, for the next couple of months, the threesome is kept very busy and involved with the tribe and village. Gabriel is the mastermind; with John's assistance, he constructs a modest medical building, develops an irrigation system, and builds a water holding tank, septic system, and sanitary system for human waste (outhouses). Even though many of the tribesmen contribute physical labor, digging pipelines and holes for in-ground holding tanks, the construction takes many weeks, even for such a small village. Gabriel learned much from previously living with the tribe when marooned on the island, and he gladly shares his knowledge.

Mary now works at the new, modestly constructed medical facility that Gabriel and John have just completed. The facility includes twenty cot-style beds, which were fortunately part of their supplies. She has Mudiwa working with her, and

Mudiwa is an excellent assistant nurse, even though she has had no formal training.

At around 3:00 p.m. on a Thursday afternoon, a mother and her six-year-old daughter enter the facility. As Mary approaches them, she sees tears in the mother's eyes and then looks down at the little girl. The young girl appears to have a fever, has abdominal pains, diarrhea, and has been vomiting. Mudiwa walks up to the mother and asks in their native language how long the girl has been sick. The mother replies that she has been slowly getting worse for around three days now.

Mudiwa takes the girl's hand and walks her over to one of the beds. She has the girl undress and put on a hospital gown, and then she puts her in bed. Mary takes her temperature, which reads 102.2 degrees. Then she puts a cool, damp cloth on her forehead. The young girl closes her eyes and quickly falls asleep.

Mary examines the girl, and though she is fully aware of the symptoms, she does not want to jump to any premature conclusions without further observation. For the entire night, Mary and Mudiwa take shifts watching the girl, cooling her body down with damp cloths and giving her medication in an attempt to break the fever.

At around 7:00 a.m. the next morning, a man

walks into the medical facility with his wife, who looks to be quite ill. Mary meets the couple and immediately sees that the woman is in need of medical attention.

As they discuss her symptoms, Mary realizes that the woman has the same exact ailments as the little girl. Mudiwa walks the woman over to one of the beds, where she has her disrobe, put on a hospital gown, and lies down. The woman also has a temperature of 102.8 degrees and needs to be cooled down with damp cloths and medication.

Within the next six hours, five more individuals come to the medical facility, and all have the same symptoms. Mary is now certain and extremely concerned that they all have the Ebola Zaire virus and is fully aware of what a contagious virus could do, as she saw many deaths while working at the Royal North Shore Hospital in Lamin, Guinea.

Ebola Zaire is one of the scariest virus species in nature, with a death rate of nine out of ten infected. Ebola Zaire is contagious through bodily fluids, but it is still unknown if it can be transferred through indirect or airborne contact.

Within the next twenty-four hours, the medical facility is filled to capacity with patients having the exact same symptoms and ailments. Mary and Mudiwa are overwhelmed, and Gabriel and

John are now also assisting with the needed nursing duties. John, who was previously a medic in the military and in the Merchant Marines, is an immense help to Mary, as he is familiar and comfortable in working under these conditions.

As he and Mary discuss the situation, John says to Mary, "This is getting out of control. We cannot handle any more patients and have just run out of beds."

Mary says to John, "The Ebola Zaire virus has always been thought to only be transferred through bodily fluids. However, we now know that this is incorrect, because all of these people would not be exposed through just bodily fluids, considering one is a young child. As far as taking on any more patients, we have no choice but to have them lie on bedding on the floor. They must all be contained in this building so as not to spread the virus to any more people."

Mary, John and Gabriel were inoculated. However, but the treatment is experimental, and no proven treatment or vaccine currently exists. For the next several days, all four work around the clock, with little sleep. They are exhausted, and each takes short naps when possible.

It is the fifth day now, and Mary is concerned, as Mudiwa, John, and herself are now showing early signs of the virus. Mary informs Gabriel what she is observing and calls John over to their private meeting. When discussing this with John, he indicates he has also noticed the symptoms and is concerned for all of them. However, Gabriel has not yet shown any symptoms and now has a look of deep concern and despair on his face. Mary advises Gabriel on what he should do if they become very ill with the virus and that he will know within two days, as, typically, the virus shows its ugly face within seven days. Hopefully, their inoculation will now begin to work and will get them through this early period of the virus.

CHAPTER 31

For the next twenty-four hours, they all continue to nurse the very ill. However, it is becoming increasingly difficult for Mary, John, and Mudiwa to keep focused, and they are becoming noticeably weaker.

It is now the beginning of the seventh day. Mary wakes up from her short nap, walks into the open bay with all of the patients, and sees Mudiwa lying face down on the floor. Mary runs over to her and sees that she is unconscious. Mary gets down on her knees, elevates Mudiwa's head, and can see that her face is bright red and hot with fever.

Mary calls out, and John hears her words and quickly comes out of the back room to see what is going on. He leaves and soon returns with damp, cool washcloths, and he places them on Mudiwa's forehead to try and cool her down. After washing her face and neck, John and Mary look at each other and see that they too have flushed faces and it is obvious that they are fully infected. Gabriel enters the room and sees Mary and John with Mudiwa and quickly walks over to them. As Gabriel looks at Mary and John, it is obvious that they have the virus.

Mary informs Gabriel that there is nothing that

can be done at this point and asks that he help them onto air mattresses that are located in the back room of the facility. As Gabriel carries Mudiwa to a mattress, Mary and John slowly follow.

When Mary is lying on the mattress, with Gabriel sitting next to her, she looks up at him, strokes his cheek with her hand, and, with teary eyes, says, "I love you, as you are the light of my life. God, in His wisdom, has saved you, as you have still a greater purpose in life and have not yet performed all that God has planned for you."

As Gabriel looks down on Mary, his eyes instantly fill with tears, and he says, "Mary, I can save you."

Mary says, "No. Your healing abilities have proven to be one on one, as you have saved others and me in the past. If all of the sick cannot be saved and healed, then I do not want to be singled out, as I am no better or more deserving than all of the sick that are with us."

Gabriel leans down, strokes her face with his hand, and kisses her right cheek. Mary's tears are now flowing down her cheeks.

She says, "I love you, Gabriel. Thank you for loving me and sharing your life with me. I love and believe in Jesus as my Savior, and I am not afraid to die, just saddened that I must now leave you. Please, pray for all of us, as I know God will hear your prayer."

With a slight smile on her face, Mary closes her eyes and takes her last breath. Gabriel covers his face with his hands, cries out loud, and has an empty feeling in his heart similar to when Mary died in the limousine accident years ago. As Gabriel is crying and in deep depression, a thought flashes through his mind. He stands up, walks over to a clear glass pitcher of water and just stares down at it. As he is leaning over the container, he can see his facial reflection in the still water and illuminated on his forehead is the sign of a cross. Gabriel's red tears of blood now drop into the water.

Within seconds, a whirlpool is created in the water, and then shortly thereafter, a strong whirlwind blows throughout the entire room. The swirling wind in the room is surreal, and to Gabriel, it appears to be in slow motion. As the wind subsides, Gabriel takes a chalice from the shelf and fills it with the red water. He then walks over to Mary, anoints a few drops of water on her forehead, stares down at her, gets down on his knees, bows his head, and begins a silent prayer over her.

"Dear Christ, my heavenly father, I am asking You to please hear my prayer. Christ, I love and believe in You with all my heart and soul. As You know, Mary, who is my loving wife, has just passed, and I don't know if I can continue on without her. She is my life's partner and confidant, and I need her to hold my hand and guide me here on earth. Christ, Mary loves and believes in You, and I ask that You please return her to me so that we can be together to work hand in hand to help the less fortunate and teach Your word of love and everlasting life. God, in Your infinite wisdom, whatever You decide, I will respectfully agree to. Thank You, Christ, for being my loving God. In Jesus' name, I pray."

Within ten seconds, Mary's blue eyes slowly open, and the first thing she sees is Gabriel's face. She smiles and says, "Gabriel, I just had a dream that I was in Heaven with Jesus. I saw His face, and Heaven is the most beautiful, peaceful, and loving place you could ever imagine. There was no feeling of fear, despair, or pain, and all of the questions I have ever had have now been answered. My life flashed before me, and everything made sense. Gabriel, I have been truly blessed, and my life now has been changed forever. I have always loved and believed in Jesus, but now, having experienced this wonderful event, I now have a complete understanding of life and purpose."

Mary leans forward, up from the air mattress, as Gabriel meets her halfway. They embrace and kiss, and both are crying, not just from Mary being saved but also for the love of Jesus. With Gabriel's assistance, Mary gets up from the mattress and begins to assist Gabriel with anointing the holy water on John, then Mudiwa, and finally on all of the infected patients. The scene in the hospital is unbelievable, as, within a short period of time, all of the patients are out of bed, standing, smiling, walking, and embracing one another. It is truly a miracle, what has just occurred, and everyone present knows that they have been saved.

After a short period of time, everyone begins to leave the hospital and pass by Gabriel, who is standing by the front door. As they pass Gabriel one by one, they bow, kiss his hand, and thank him for saving them. Mary and John, who are standing next to Gabriel, just smile at him.

Gabriel then says, "I truly hope these people understand that I did not save them, that only God can perform such a miracle. I am merely God's messenger and only doing what God has requested of me."

CHAPTER 32

Within a few days' time, the news of a "Healer" has drawn literally hundreds of people from all over the region. People arrive in droves to see who this person might be. Some of the curious have walked day and night to see for themselves that a person who performs miracles is for real.

At the village, the number of people arriving overwhelms Gabriel, Mary, and John, and Gabriel is not sure how to handle the situation, as they are not prepared for such an onslaught. In deep thought, Gabriel realizes that this is the perfect time to speak to all of the visitors and express the truth that is in his heart.

With the assistance of John and some of the village tribesmen, they construct a platform where Gabriel can be elevated so he can easily be heard and seen by all in attendance. Within one hour, the platform is constructed, and all of the people crowd in front of the stage with much curiosity. As Gabriel now steps up on the platform, the large crowd becomes immediately silent, with all eyes fixed upon him.

As Gabriel looks over the small sea of people, he sees mothers holding their babies, brothers, sisters, husbands, neighbors, and people from many different tribes all standing shoulder to shoulder. In fact, many of the people present are feuding tribes in opposition to each other. However, at this particular time, their fear and hate is not present. They are all here for one reason only, and that is to see and hear from this so-called "Healer."

As Gabriel begins to speak, with Mudiwa acting as interpreter, it is quiet enough to hear a pin drop, even though they are outside. Then something very odd happens, something that is a surprise even to Gabriel.

As he reaches his right arm up towards the sky, a small bird lands on his shoulder, and within moments, the entire platform is covered with birds. Not just one particular species, but a large variety of birds that normally do not congregate together. Gabriel looks down, sees all of the birds, and begins to smile. With all in attendance witnessing this "Bird Show," people begin to point at the birds, smile, and speak softly about what they are witnessing.

Gabriel knows exactly what is happening, as this is a sign from God informing him that what he is doing is a good thing and that he is going to take this opportunity to become not just a preacher, but also a teacher about Jesus and God.

For the next sixty minutes, Gabriel tells the

story about Jesus' life, the circumstances of His birth, when He was a boy, the miracles that He performed, and how He died on the cross for all of our sins. He then goes on to say that if you have Jesus in your heart and follow His words of wisdom, to love yourself and your neighbor, that you will have everlasting life. Gabriel's presentation and words are so moving that many in attendance are sobbing and wiping their eyes, and even Mary and John have tear-filled eyes just listening to the words and love that Gabriel expresses from his heart.

After Gabriel completes his presentation, he invites everyone to the river, where he can perform a mass baptismal. When all are in the water, Gabriel, Mary, and John walk through the crowd and anoint people's heads with the river water.

After all have been anointed, Gabriel raises his hand and says the words, "I baptize you in the name of the Father, and of the Son, and of the Holy Spirit."

Gabriel then says, "Will you please introduce yourself and either embrace or shake the hand of someone that you do NOT know so they can be your new extended spiritual family member."

This leads to quite a scene, as hundreds of people smile and embrace one another. Gabriel hopes that this will create a bond between the tribes to no longer hate and harm one another and to respect their fellow man and woman in the name of Jesus Christ. After all is finally done, Gabriel stands on the shoreline and greets and shakes the hand of every single person that is present as they depart the river.

As the last person leaves Gabriel, Mary and John are tired and hungry and decide to go back to the village, have some dinner, and retire early, as this has been an exhausting and enriching day for them.

CHAPTER 33

That same evening, and in the middle of the night, as Gabriel lies in bed looking up at the dark ceiling, he is restless and cannot sleep. He quietly gets up, so as to not wake Mary, and gets dressed.

He walks out to the fire pit and gazes into the fire, which is in full flame, as it is a tribal custom that the fire must never go out from dusk to dawn. This is an ancient belief that the fire will ward off evil spirits at night while all are at rest.

Gabriel gazes into the fire, and it is as if he has become hypnotized by the blue, red, and orange colors of the flames. He looks deeper into the fire, losing consciousness of his surroundings, as if in a trance. As he continues to stare at the flames, he hears what appears to be a slight whisper in his right ear, though he cannot quite make out what the words are trying to say to him.

As he listens closely, the whisper becomes more discernible, and it says, "Save me. Save us all."

Gabriel quickly turns his head to the right to see who is speaking to him. It is such an eerie feeling that overcomes him that the hairs on the back of his neck actually stand up. He looks around the area but sees no one and is unsure of what has just happened.

He is suddenly overcome by a strong impulse

to venture out of the village. Before leaving, he stops by his hut and grabs a flashlight to take with him. As he walks out and away from the village, he feels guided to go in a certain direction and does not question himself. After walking for around fifteen minutes, he comes upon a clearing. It is so dark, however, that even his flashlight offers little assistance, and he is unsure of his steps.

Continuing his walk through the clearing, ahead, he sees a very dim light, and it is puzzling to him. At first, he thinks it might be a fire, but the closer he walks to the light, the more confused he becomes about what he is viewing. When he finally gets close enough, he sees that the light source is created from literally thousands of fireflies flying over and illuminating a particular area of the ground.

Gabriel stops short of this spectacle and just stares at the fantastic lightshow, watching in amazement with a big grin on his face. As he continues to watch, he is nudged into the middle of the lights, and instantly, thousands of fireflies land on his clothing and hair. Gabriel stands for a moment in the middle of the lights, and is all aglow. He looks up, and the sight is surreal. It is a portal in the sky, a colored ring, which is an actual gateway to another dimension.

As Gabriel continues to look up at the portal,

he cannot take his eyes off the colored illuminating sphere and is in awe of its beauty and mystery. Within seconds, he hears faint voices that seem to be coming from the very ground that he is standing on. Gabriel gets on his knees and puts his ear to the ground, and the voices and words become much more discernible. The sounds he hears are cries for help, and the voices are crying, "Save me. Save us all."

Gabriel looks down at the very ground that he is kneeling on and begins to panic, believing that there are people trapped beneath him. With his bare hands, he frantically starts to dig out the earth. As he continues to dig, his hands start to become raw and slightly bloody, and the dirt becomes caked under his fingernails.

Quickly, Gabriel becomes exhausted from his vigorous labor, but even with sweat pouring from his forehead and his hands in pain, he knows he cannot stop. As he continues to dig, he finally comes upon a soft area in the earth and starts to scoop the dirt rather than dig straight down. Within a short time, he makes a gruesome discovery.

As he looks down, horror immediately appears on his face. Gabriel has discovered a shallow grave, and what he is now looking at are bodies of children. The children are fully clothed and appear to have been murdered within the past couple of days.

It is a horrible sight, and Gabriel, still on his knees, holding his face in his hands, begins to cry and yells out, "WHY? Why would anyone kill these innocent children of God?"

With some reluctance, Gabriel takes the bodies out of the grave, seven in total, and places them on their backs, one beside the other. He looks down at the lifeless bodies of the children, three girls and four boys, bows his head, and says a prayer.

"Dear Christ, our Heavenly Father, I ask that You please hear my words of mercy for these children. Lord, I humbly entrust these children, so precious in Your sight. Please, take them into Your arms and welcome them into paradise, where there is no pain, sorrow, or weeping but the fullness of Your presence with joy. I pray that they will have everlasting peace with You and Your Son, Jesus Christ, forever and ever. In Your name, I pray. Amen."

As Gabriel stands above the lifeless bodies, his own body numb from the senseless loss of life, he again begins to cry, and a feeling of great depression rushes through his brain. Gabriel again drops to his knees, with eyes full of heavy tears, bows his head, and concentrates intensely with a vision of Jesus in his mind.

From above Gabriel and the children's bodies, a wind begins to blow. Gabriel, however, is unaware, as he is deep in thought. Within seconds, Gabriel hears what appears to be something in flight. He looks up to see an unbelievable appearance.

With the area still all aglow from the illumination of the fireflies, coming down from the portal are beautiful streaks of seven colored lights, the colors of the rainbow. As the lights become closer, the wind becomes stronger, so strong, in fact, that it is like a gale-force windstorm. Gabriel stands up to view the colorful spectacle, his hair and clothes blowing in the wind, and he is still unsure of what he is witnessing.

As Gabriel stands there in awe of what is occurring, the first colored light approaches from above, and suddenly it is like he is in a vacuum. All around Gabriel and the fireflies are strong winds. In their immediate area, however, it is perfectly calm. Shortly thereafter, the second, third, fourth, fifth, sixth, and seventh lights all come in contact with the children.

At first, Gabriel is somewhat puzzled by what is occurring, but he knows that his prayers are being answered. Just then, the colored lights transform into glowing angels from above, who have arrived to save the children, to take the children to Heaven so they may be with Jesus and God forever.

At this very moment in time, Gabriel is actually face to face with an angel. As he stands in awe of what is happening, all of the angels gather around him and place their hands on him. As they do this, a cross appears on his forehead, a warm, tingling sensation rushes through his body, and he immediately has loving thoughts of Jesus.

The angels go to the children and embrace them. They all transform again into lights and ascend towards the portal on their heavenly journey.

Gabriel, now with weak knees, sits down and just stares up at the portal in the sky. As he continues to watch the colors of the portal, it slowly begins to fade away. Then the fireflies begin to dissipate, and within seconds, Gabriel is sitting all alone on the ground in the dark.

Still looking up at the sky, Gabriel watches the colors of the portal completely fade away, and he knows that his journey tonight is one that God planned for him. It was unfortunate and very sad that the children had died, but Gabriel freed them from their earthly prison, and they were saved by the grace of God.

In the dark, Gabriel stands up and looks for his flashlight, which is lying on the ground just a few feet away. As he bends over to pick up the flashlight, his back is sore, his hands slightly bloody, and his body is as tired as if he had just completed an intense workout. With stiff legs, tender hands and fingers, and aching back, Gabriel slowly returns to the village, gets back into bed, and quickly falls into a deep REM sleep, as he is completely exhausted.

CHAPTER 34

The next morning, Mary dresses and does her morning chores while Gabriel sleeps in due to his exhausting adventure the night before. This, of course, is quite unusual, as Gabriel is always the first one up in the morning, either planning the day's events or completing a job from the previous day. As Mary walks back into their darkened hut, she is a little concerned and sees that Gabriel is now finally waking.

Gabriel looks up at Mary, smiles, and says, "Good morning. What time is it?"

Mary tells him that he has slept in, but she does not know the hour, as they usually do not live their daily lives in the village by any particular time frame, which is much different from the civilized world.

Gabriel throws the covers back and sits up in bed. His back is sore, his hands and fingers are slightly raw, and his legs are a little unstable. Mary watches him with a peculiar look on her face, saying nothing. Gabriel stands and stretches, and as he attempts to loosen up his body, Mary just stands there, staring directly at him.

Gabriel slowly puts on his shirt, pants, socks,

and shoes. Once dressed, he sits down on the bed, falls back, and just lies there with apparently little energy.

Mary says, "Gabriel, are you alright? I have never seen you with this lack of energy or enthusiasm."

Gabriel sits up and tells Mary about what happened the night before. As he completes his story, he has tears in his eyes, for the children and also for the blessed event with the angels. She has many questions, and for the next ten minutes, Gabriel answers her in great detail.

Once Mary's questions have been answered, Gabriel stands up from the bed, Mary approaches him, and they hug. As they separate from their embrace, Mary is now within inches of Gabriel's face, her face now with a perplexed look. She stares into his eyes, takes her right hand, and gently strokes his face.

She stares at Gabriel, thoughts run through her mind, and she becomes instantly panicked and unsure of what she is witnessing. She takes Gabriel's hand and walks him out of the hut into the sunlight. As they stand there, Mary turns and looks directly at Gabriel and stares without expression.

As Gabriel stands there looking down at Mary, he can see the tears in her eyes. A puzzled look grows on his face. Mary takes her right hand, gently strokes his face, and, losing control, breaks down and cries.

Gabriel, not sure of what is happening, says, "Mary, what is it?"

As Mary again looks up at Gabriel, she sees the face of an aged man, with gray hair and the physique of a much older person. She says, "Gabriel, you were in direct contact with holiness last night. When the angels touched you, you were blessed. However, this has changed your physical appearance and has aged you. This is the recognition you have received for doing God's work."

Gabriel immediately walks back into the hut, takes a mirror out of Mary's bag, and again walks out into the sunlight. As he looks in the mirror, he is surprised at his appearance and says nothing.

He then smiles at Mary and says, "I have been blessed throughout my life, and this slight physical transformation is just a reminder of how frail we are as human beings. I honor my new physical appearance, as it is God's recognition to me that I completed his blessings last night."

The two hug. For the rest of the day, they continue to perform their normal duties and responsibilities.

CHAPTER 35

For the next few months, life in the village is quite normal. However, Mary notices that Gabriel's physical appearance has continued to age, and his energy level has continued to decrease since his experience with the angels. She does not mention this to him, but she knows that he has noticed the difference.

One early evening, around dusk, with a full moon above, Gabriel and Mary sit on a large rock down by the stream, which is where they spend their private time.

Mary takes Gabriel's hand and says, "I have something that I want to share with you."

As Gabriel looks at Mary, he can see her eyes are teary and magically twinkling. The moonlight reflects off the water, giving Mary's face the radiance and glow of an angel.

She then squeezes his hand, smiles, and says, with tears slowly flowing down her cheeks, "Gabriel, you are going to be a father."

Gabriel looks into Mary's face, stunned. Then he tears up, smiles, and gives her a hug like no other.

"Oh my God, are you sure?"

She tells him that she sent her pregnancy test

to the local medical center two weeks earlier and just received the confirmation.

Gabriel, now all excited, says, "What am I supposed to do?"

She says, "For a while, everything will be as normal. However, I want to have our child born at home in the States with our parents present."

Gabriel replies, "That is exactly what we will do, and until then, you must take good care of yourself and not overdo things."

They then walk back to the village and see John sitting by the fire. As they approach John, hand in hand and smiling, he knows immediately what is happening.

He looks at them, smiles, and says, "You both have a look of joy on your faces. Is there something that you want to tell me?"

Mary grabs John's hand and says, "Gabriel is going to be a father."

John looks at Mary and says, "And you are going to be a mother."

He stands, and the three hug, and no one could be happier for them than John, as he is their closest friend. As all three then sit around the fire and talk, Gabriel tells John that Mary will be delivering the baby at home in the States and will be returning in five months.

John then informs them that he, too, also has something to share with them. "I will be soon permanently going back to the States."

Gabriel looks at John in disappointment and asks if he has done something wrong.

John looks at Gabriel, smiles, and says, "You and Mary are not only my best friends but are my surrogate family. I have just received a letter of acceptance from OHSU medical school in Oregon to start my schooling to become a doctor. I want to become a family practitioner and start my own practice to assist the underprivileged and less fortunate, those that are in need of real, free medical attention. I want it to become a non-profit medical facility. Gabriel and Mary, these past sixteen months that we have worked and lived together have taught me so much about what really matters in life. Gabriel, God has blessed you with amazing abilities, and the love of Christ in your heart is immeasurable. You have truly been chosen by God to perform his work here on earth. Mary, ever since you and Gabriel first met in kindergarten, God's plan was for you to be his partner in life and also to perform God's work. There are not two more loving and giving people on this earth. Before we met, my life was empty and self-absorbed, and I had no belief in Christ. You have enriched my soul, and the love of life for myself and others has taken me to a place that is as high as Heaven, and I thank you for that."

John then breaks down and begins to sob like a child and puts his hands over his face. His tears are not only for his friendship with Gabriel and Mary, but also for his love of Jesus. Gabriel, Mary, and John then again embrace one another. Gabriel knows that John has been transformed and the love in his heart will guide him on his upcoming journey in life.

CHAPTER 36

As time continues, John departs and goes back to the States to pursue his studies. Gabriel and Mary feel a void in their lives without John's presence and continue their daily lives.

Mary is now definitely showing and has a beautiful glow about her. Her duties at the village have changed, as she must be careful not to overexert herself or do anything dangerous. Gabriel keeps a keen eye on her to make sure she is safe. Mary gets a big kick out of Gabriel as he pampers her. Mary, being a nurse, knows exactly what she needs to do to keep herself safe and in good health and allows Gabriel to pretend to be in charge.

Finally, it is time for them to depart for the States, as Mary is now into the seventh month of her pregnancy. As they bid their good-byes to the villagers they have come to know and love, they meet out in the landing for the single-engine Cessna 172M, which is the same type of plane that originally brought them. As the plane lands, the pilot walks out, around the aircraft, and they make eye contact.

To their disbelief, it is the same pilot who calls himself Sky King who will be flying them back to Kigali. Sky King offers his hand in greeting but takes a double look at Gabriel, as he remembers what he looked like less than two years ago. They all smile, exchange pleasantries, and load the plane with their luggage and small mementos that the villagers have made in thanks for their support.

After the plane leaves the ground and is in flight, the pilot circles the village and swoops down and waves his wings at all of the villagers who are looking up and waving good-bye. Looking down at the villagers, Gabriel and Mary both get a sad feeling knowing that they are leaving friends and a temporary home and will never again return. This has been a good adventure for them, and they have learned a lot, not just about village living and the people, but also about themselves.

The flight, for the most part, is smooth, with some occurring turbulence, and they are in flight for approximately two hours. When they arrive at Kigali airport, it is Chinedu that is waiting for them outside on the runway with his extended cab truck adjacent to the loading dock.

As Chinedu walks up to the Cessna, he first sees Mary and gives her a hug and then walks up to Gabriel, who is unloading their luggage. He then taps Gabriel on this shoulder, and Gabriel turns and looks Chinedu in the eye. As Chinedu looks at Gabriel, he is quite surprised at his appearance. However, he smiles, and they hug one another.

In an instant, a young girl exits the truck and walks over to Chinedu and Gabriel. As Gabriel looks down on the young girl, he recognizes her, as it is Chinwendu, Chinedu's daughter that he healed two years ago. She is now taller and looks a lot like her father. As Gabriel kneels down to be at eye level with her, she looks into Gabriel's eyes, and tears gently flow down her cheeks. She then puts her arms around Gabriel's neck and hugs him and does not let go.

She whispers into Gabriel's ear, "Thank you for saving me."

Gabriel whispers back, "It was God who saved you."

They continue to embrace for a few more seconds, and then she walks over to her dad's side and holds his hand.

After loading the luggage onto the truck, they take it to the airlines and have an early luggage drop off, which makes it easier for them at departure. They then go to a restaurant in the airport, have lunch, and discuss all that is going on in their lives. Time passes, and as their flight is scheduled to depart around 4:00 p.m., they bid their farewells and invite Chinedu and his family to visit them in the states.

They board Kenya Airlines Flight #1219,

depart on time, and fly to Nairobi, and after a two-hour layover, they board United Airlines Flight #427 and fly to Amsterdam. After a three-hour layover, they again board United Airlines Flight #930 directly to Portland and then arrive late the next day. It was a long flight, and they are extremely glad to be back home.

Meeting them at the airport are both Gabriel and Mary's parents, and they are all very happy to see one another. Mary notices that all of the parents are staring at Gabriel, but she says nothing.

CHAPTER 37

For the next four weeks, both families have more than enough time to talk and ask questions about their stay in Rwanda. The stories told are quite fascinating about the African natives, their lifestyles, health issues, beliefs, myths, and outlook on life in general. Even though they were halfway around the world and lived in completely different cultures and environments, the family problems and emotions to their problems were remarkably similar to ours in the States.

As Mary is entering into her ninth month, she, Sarah, and Pamela are at Lloyd Center Mall doing some light shopping for their soon-to-be grandchild. While at Macy's, sales associate Connie notices Mary is looking a little flushed and escorts her to a nearby chair. As Mary sits and rests on the chair, she begins to get lightheaded, and her face becomes bright red. Mary's mother Pamela looks directly at Mary and sees that she does not look well. Then, at that very moment, Mary's water breaks, and she just sits there as if in shock and embarrassed. She then regains her composure, as, being a nurse, she knows exactly how to handle this situation, and she tells her mother that they must take her to Providence Hospital, which is just fifteen minutes away.

They contact Lloyd Center security, and with the assistance of Bret, the security guard, put her in a wheelchair and then transport her to the emergency section at the hospital. She is then brought to the maternity ward, and while resting comfortably in her private room, in walks Gabriel with a look of concern on his face. Mary is lying down and resting in labor. She looks up at Gabriel as he approaches her bed, and they both smile. Gabriel then grabs Mary's hand and kisses her gently on her right cheek.

As his lips touch Mary's face, he notices how soft her skin feels and how beautiful she looks in her pregnant state. At this exact moment, he has a flashback to when he visited Mary the night she was to go to the senior prom with Chad. How beautiful she looked, and it was at that exact moment that Gabriel knew he loved Mary.

For the next couple of hours, Gabriel stays with Mary as her contractions increase and her cervix is now dilated to above seven cm. Now Pamela enters the room, accompanied by Dr. Taylor, who is to be the delivery doctor.

The doctor walks up to Mary's bedside, smiles and grabs her hand, and asks her how she is feeling. Mary replies that she is experiencing much more pain now and her contractions are increasing. He then explains to her exactly what his procedure will be during the delivery. Mary completely understands what the procedure will be, as she was also an attending nurse in the delivery room while in Africa.

Within a few more minutes, the contractions are now rapid, and she has dilated to ten cm and is ready to deliver their child. Gabriel is already dressed in a gown and mask and is awaiting Mary's arrival in the operating room. As Mary is brought into the delivery room, she is in considerable discomfort and does not notice that Gabriel is present. She then asks the nurse to please find Gabriel.

Gabriel walks up to her bedside, grabs her hand, and says, "Sweetheart, I am here."

Mary turns her head, sees Gabriel above her, and asks him to say a prayer. Gabriel looks at everyone in attendance, they all bow their heads, and he says, "Dear Lord, our Heavenly Father, please grant skill and wisdom to the doctors and nurses that will be taking care of Mary and delivering our child today. Jesus, thank You for this new gift of life that You will bestow on us. Whatever happens, Lord, I know that it is in Your heavenly design. I know that You will never leave or forsake us. Father, we humbly give our baby to You. May our child grow up to follow Your teachings throughout their life and guide us as loving parents. In Jesus' name, I pray. Amen."

As Dr. Taylor is now at the foot of the bed and the attending nurses are on both sides of the bed, Gabriel is at Mary's side, giving her the Lamaze instruction that was taught in classes since they arrived back from Rwanda. Gabriel watches and listens intensely to everything that is occurring and instructing Mary when to breathe. With everyone wearing their masks, it is difficult to read expressions on how the delivery is going. However, no one appears to be overly concerned, as this is just another day at the office for these professionals.

Dr. Taylor now instructs Mary to push (bear down), which helps move the baby through the birth canal. He instructs her to take a breath at the beginning of every contraction, hold it, and push, which tightens the abdominal muscles and exert as much pressure as possible. While this continues, the nurse then counts to ten. Then he again instructs Mary to take a quick breath and push for another count of ten, trying to get three pushes in for each contraction. As this procedure continues, the doctor looks at Gabriel and tells him that this pushing stage can last for a few minutes to several hours.

After about another twenty minutes, the baby's head is crowning, and Mary is now instructed to stop pushing to avoid tearing. It is a very intense time for Mary, Gabriel, and, of course, the baby. The doctor now says that the baby's head is out of the vagina. However, he pauses and just stares at the child's head with a look of disbelief painted on his face. As he is staring down at the child's head, he sees what appears to be a Red Cross on the baby's forehead, but he says nothing, and within seconds, the baby's entire body is delivered.

Dr. Taylor takes a short pause as he examines the baby. However, now he does not see any physical appearance on the baby's forehead. At this particular time, the doctor does not clamp the umbilical cord, as recent research has found that cutting the cord too early denies the babies of an important supply of blood and can possibly reduce the supply of iron that a baby needs. After several minutes, the doctor cuts the umbilical cord.

Without any reservation, he says, "Congratulations, you are now the parents of a beautiful baby girl," but he does not mention to anyone what he has witnessed. As he cradles the child, he slightly elevates his arms so that both Mary and Gabriel can see their beautiful baby.

The nurse wraps the baby in a towel and lays the child down beside Mary, and Gabriel leans in to get a first-hand view. As they now are in awe of their new creation, they both have intense smiles, with tears flowing down their cheeks. The nurse takes the child from Mary and says she will deliver their baby to her hospital room as soon as Mary arrives. Gabriel thanks everyone in attendance for their professionalism and gives Dr. Taylor a hug.

The doctor walks over to the nurse who is attending to the child and just stares at the baby. As the nurse notices the special attention Dr. Taylor is giving to the child, she has a perplexed look on her face and says, "Doctor, is everything OK?"

Dr. Taylor says nothing, but he continues to stare at the child, and then he rubs his finger over the child's forehead and feels and sees nothing.

Again, the nurse asks, "Is everything OK?"

Dr. Taylor then says, "Yes, it appears that all is OK." He then departs the operating room, and the nurse continues to clean the child.

Shortly thereafter, the baby is brought to Mary's private room and is greeted by two very proud parents. Within minutes, both Mary and Gabriel's parents enter the room with big smiles and surround the bed, all wanting to have the first look at their beautiful new grandchild.

For the next few hours, Gabriel and Mary are considering some names for their new daughter, and it is more difficult for them than they imagined. After considerable thought, they both agree on the name, Olivia. The biblical connotation of Olivia is the olive tree, which is a symbol of fruitfulness, beauty, and dignity. The extending of an olive branch signifies an offer of peace.

CHAPTER 38

It is now two months later, and Gabriel and Mary have been very busy attending to their new daughter and daily schedules. Mary's other main concern is for Gabriel, as he has not been feeling well, has not been himself, and she has noticed that his aging still appears to be accelerating. Gabriel is fully aware of his physical appearance and also that his memory is not as sharp as it was just three months ago.

This particular Sunday is to be a grand day in their lives, as Olivia is to be baptized. As they enter the foyer of the church, they are greeted by Pastor Maragelis, who is the same pastor that baptized Gabriel. The church is also the same one that Gabriel was baptized in and that his family has attended for many years, and it holds many memories.

As all in attendance are seated in the pews, Pastor Maragelis walks in, stands at his podium, looks down and out at his congregation, smiles, and graciously welcomes everyone. For the first couple of minutes, he speaks about Christianity and spirituality. He then defines the purpose of baptism and its significant meaning in each of our lives. The baptismal ritual (Christening or Sacrament) is the gateway to life and spirit and to be freed from the power of darkness and brought into the realm of freedom of the children of God.

Pastor Maragelis then steps down from the altar and approaches the baptismal. He then instructs Gabriel and Mary, who has Olivia cradled in her arms, and the witnesses, who are all four parents, to please join him. As they are standing around the baptismal, the pastor instructs Mary to remove the linen cloth from Olivia's head.

The pastor now looks down on the child's exposed head, takes a gold shell in his right hand, anoints her head with the holy water (affusion), and states, "Olivia Melina Adams, in the presence of Our Lord God and Jesus Christ, I baptize you in the name of the Father, Son, and Holy Ghost." He then repeats the words and anointing of the child a second and third time. The three anointing's mean when Jesus went into the wild for forty days and forty nights and was tested by the devil three times.

After the third anointing, some of the holy water trickles down on Olivia's forehead, and only Gabriel notices. However, he lets the holy water remain. As he continues to stare at the water on her forehead, he notices that the water turns blood red, and then a Red Cross appears. He touches her forehead with his right index finger, and an immediate warming sensation rushes to his brain and then throughout his entire body. At that very moment, Gabriel's body goes numb, he begins to get dizzy and lightheaded, his legs lose strength and balance, and he collapses to the floor.

As Gabriel's father, Joseph, immediately attempts to assist him, he can see that Gabriel is not breathing and begins CPR, which he is fully trained to administer. As he continues CPR, he can see that Gabriel's face is turning blue and that he is not getting oxygen to his lungs and brain. After a few more minutes of intense CPR, everyone around Gabriel can see that his body is lifeless and his green eyes have turned to a lifeless, dull gray in color.

As Gabriel is unconscious, he enters into an out-of-body dream state. His sensation is surreal, but also one of wonderment. In his vision, his body feels weightless, and his surroundings are dark. As he continues, he can feel the wind in his face as though he is being transported. He then sees a small light ahead, which seems to get larger and brighter as he continues. To Gabriel, he senses that he is in some sort of universal wormhole and time travel is taking him to a place that he is now very anxious to observe. Gabriel can feel himself smiling with a sense of euphoria. There is no sense of time but just of extreme calmness.

In an instant, he approaches a blinding bright light and then sees nothing but blue. It is sky blue, and he is above the landscape of where? As he now observes his hands and arms and then his torso, he can see that he is transparent. He can feel himself breathing and knows that his body is there but in a completely different realm of existence. It is not one of blood, bones, skin, and skeletal structure, but one of pure energy. What an exotic feeling this is, knowing in your mind that you exist, but in a completely different concept.

Gabriel has an overwhelming feeling that he has been here before, but how can this be? This is a place like no other and certainly not like earth. Gabriel wonders and is perplexed about where and what this new environment must be. Then, in an instant, he is approached by a figure that he thinks he recognizes. It appears to be an angel smiling and extending a hand of friendship and comfort.

There is no verbal communication needed, as the thought process is completely telepathic. As Gabriel accompanies the angel, he is in wonderment of what he is next to experience. Suddenly, he is completely surrounded by what appears to be brightly colored lights of energy. As he stands in amazement and in awe of his surroundings, his mind commands him to get on his knees and bow his head. With bowed head, he slowly looks forward and upward. The bright light of energy is so intense and blinding that he cannot look directly at the figure.

Then, in his mind, he hears a voice communicating with him. It is a voice that he thinks he recognizes from his dreams but not one he expects to hear while supposedly conscious.

Communicating telepathically, Gabriel asks, "Where am I, and why am I here?"

The answer comes back to him: "You are on a higher plain of consciousness, and you have been brought here to experience what is true reality as a reward for believing in Jesus as your Savior. Do you have a question for me, Gabriel?"

Gabriel replies, "There is one thing on earth that has been troubling me my entire life, and that is 'Why is there so much evil and hatred of mankind on earth?'"

The voice replies, "Evil is just the absence of God. In the mortal design of each individual, God has graced everyone born with free will. On earth, each person is a spiritual being having a human experience. Humans have been granted the freedom to live their lives and to choose which path to follow. Do you take the path of evil, greed, and lack of morality and empathy for our earthly neighbors, or do you follow God's plan to be kind, generous, to love and live in harmony, and to worship Jesus and God? It is everyone's individual choice how to live their lives and either be a non-believer or believe in Jesus as your Savior. The reward for believing in Jesus as your Savior is everlasting life. Either you truly feel Christ in your heart and ask forgiveness for your daily sins or continue on in your life hoping that all will be okay."

Gabriel thinks how lonely and sad a person must feel without Jesus in their heart. Gabriel then is instructed to teach about Jesus, as He is truly the Son of God. By his teachings, those followers who have true belief in Jesus will be rewarded by entering the kingdom of God.

Gabriel then asks, "Why do I feel like I have been in Heaven before? Is it because our souls were created in Heaven prior to our creation?"

The voice says, "When we are born on earth, God tests us to see if we are truly worthy of His glory. It is God's plan, and we are just following a script that has been written for us. Once a person is born with their soul, they now have been granted free will of their own destiny. It is up to that individual what path to take and to decide what kind of a person they will become. If they truly believe in Jesus as their Savior, then when the earthly body dies, their soul will return home to Heaven. No one truly dies. They are just transformed."

In shock, Mary is still cradling Olivia in her arms. She gets down on her knees and cries out with intense sorrow. As she bows her head down so that her face is touching Gabriel's, Olivia's eyes open wide, a Red Cross appears on her forehead, and her red tears gently drop onto Gabriel's face and forehead. At that exact moment, the wind begins to blow over Gabriel's head, with his hair swirling. Then a high wind blows throughout the entire church, and everyone in attendance experiences what appears to be an internal windstorm.

As the high wind continues to blow out of nowhere, a light flashes upward toward the cathedral ceiling, and seven lights appear. These are the same colors of the rainbow that Gabriel saw during his holy experience with the seven deceased children and fireflies.

As the colors hover above Gabriel, the interior of the church is illuminated so brightly that all in attendance must shield their eyes with their hands. Just then, a Red Cross appears on Gabriel's forehead, and a gasp of breath is heard. Mary looks down at Gabriel, and she can see that he is again breathing and his youthful physical appearance has returned. Mary smiles with tear-filled eyes and gently kisses his right cheek in sincere happiness.

From outside the church and extending down from the heavens and into the church is a bright rainbow. Neighbors and people passing by all stop in amazement to view the beautiful vibrant colors. Also, at this time, a television station crew just happens to pass by. They stop, and the camera crew videos the sensation, which will appear on the five o'clock news.

The wind now subsides, and the rainbow colors vanish in an instant, and Mary knows that the wind was the Breath of God and the rainbow colors were angels sent from Heaven. She then looks down at her cradled child, sees the Red Cross on her forehead, and knows that through the grace of God, Olivia has saved Gabriel's life. Olivia has also been blessed like Gabriel and now wonders what challenges and miracles she will experience in her life.

What future events will Gabriel, Mary and Olivia have together as being blessed and touched by the hand of God?